15 Minutes with God for Grandma

Emilie Barnes

HARVEST HOUSE PUBLISHERS

EUGENE, OREGON

Cover by Terry Dugan Design, Minneapolis, Minnesota

15 MINUTES WITH GOD FOR GRANDMA
Copyright © 2005 by Bob and Emilie Barnes
Published by Harvest House Publishers
Eugene, Oregon 97402

Library of Congress Cataloging-in-Publication Data
Barnes, Emilie.
    15 minutes with God for grandma / Emilie Barnes.
        p. cm.
    Includes bibliographical references.
    ISBN-13: 978-0-7369-1600-4
    ISBN-10: 0-7369-1600-8
    1. Grandmothers—Prayer-books and devotions—English.   I. Title: Fifteen minutes with God for grandma.   II. Title.
    BV4847.B35   2005
    242.'6431—dc22   2005001504

Printed in the United States of America

05   06   07   08   09   10   / DP-CF /   10   9   8   7   6   5   4   3   2   1

Dedicated to grandmothers who want to contribute in a positive way to the raising of their grandchildren. For some that means a great contribution because you live nearby and have an occasion to see them on a regular basis. For others, the grandchildren may not live so close by and you have limited contact with them face-to-face. Regardless of the circumstances, you also need to continue to grow in your faith. As you grow spiritually, you will become a better person, thus making you a better grandparent.

God's Blessing,

Emilie Barnes

Introduction

$\mathcal{W}$hether grandparenting is new to you or it's old hat with many grandchildren and even, in some cases, great-grand-children, these encouraging stories and illustrations of how God continues to work in our lives will uplift you and draw you closer to Him.

In the devotion sections, you'll find a verse of Scripture along with a short story of how God can work in your life, followed by a simple prayer to incorporate the day's teaching in your life. Next comes an "Action" thought that encourages you to apply today's teaching, and finally an inspirational thought under "Today's Wisdom."

"From Grammy's Kitchen" sections are simple recipes that can be used when the grandchildren come to visit. They are selected for ease in making and have been taste-tested by youngsters. So much learning and sharing takes place around food preparation. What a special time you can have with your grandchildren!

The "Spirit Lifter" sections are suggested activities that will help you be proactive in this all-important phase of your life. They will get you off the couch and out from in front of the television so you can enrich your mind and stretch your muscles.

You will also note that there are three boxes at the top of each devotion. These boxes are for you to keep track of what you have read previously. Just put a check mark in a box to show you have read it. If you read it again, place another check mark in the second or eventually the third box. This book doesn't have to be read from front to back. You are free to randomly read through the book.

As you read these devotions, may you truly look upon them as a gift from me to you. Each one has been written from my or my family's experiences and is passed on to you with love. My prayer is that you will think about what you read and put it into practice. As James says, "We are to be doers of the Word, and not merely hearers" (James 1:22). May you become a spiritually richer, more relaxed, balanced, purposeful, and loving grandparent.

Be Still

∾∾

Be still, and know that I am God.
PSALM 46:10 NIV

$\mathcal{B}$E STILL, AND KNOW THAT I AM GOD." Easier said than done, isn't it? It's hard to find a quiet moment in the day—a few minutes to relax and think and pray. Even as grandparents we're constantly on the move, pressured by demands of work and family, church involvement, community activities, and whatever recreation we can fit in. Moments to be still with God just don't happen with full schedules. Even with not having children's schedules to fit our lives around, we find ourselves overtaxed with things to do. We often ask ourselves, "How did we get everything done when we had full-time jobs and raised our children?"

So what's the solution? We must make appointments with ourselves if we are to have a chance to rest, plan, regroup, and draw closer to God!

My Bob and I just returned from five days in San Diego during the middle of summer. The temperature was perfect, 83 degrees and no humidity. There's something calming about the waves crashing on the shore. We acted like tourists. We walked, talked, ate, took a harbor tour, went to the zoo, and toured the Midway aircraft carrier. One afternoon we talked about family, ministry, goals, God's love, His Word, and our writing. Now we're both quiet, and we're feeling that rare sense of stillness the psalmist talks about.

Our lives aren't usually like this. Often our lives aren't in balance. It's easy to be more outwardly focused than inwardly focused. Goals and deadlines, coping with stress, taking care of daily chores, working toward retirement—we can spend more time and energy on these things than we do on praying, meditating on God's Word, listening to His direction, dreaming, and just being in God's presence.

As we get older, it becomes a bit easier to concentrate on the inward things. I find I sincerely desire to glorify God more with my life now. I want to know Him better. I want Him to use me. And I want to better know His peace and stillness. You probably want those things for yourself as well.

Satan doesn't want us to take the time to be still with God. And he doesn't make it easy for us to eliminate the distractions of jobs, stress from the boss, family responsibilities, ringing phones, and doing what the children and grandchildren want and need. It's a battle to make time for rest. When Bob and I set up the year's calendar, we set aside blocks of time to be alone and quiet. In-between the speaking engagements, interviews, and travel, we make time to be still. Our marriage demands it; our walk with God requires it.

The door of stillness is waiting for any of us to open it, but it won't open by itself. We have to choose to turn the knob, and then we choose to make time to enter and sit for awhile. All of us need to learn to balance the time we spend in quiet and calm with the time we spend in the fray of everyday existence. Ecclesiastes 3:1 says there is a time for everything—and that includes a time to be still despite our busy lives.

❦❦❦

PRAYER

*F*ather God, I struggle to take a time out. I know I can better serve You when I have a daily time with You. Show me how to make this happen regularly. Amen.

ACTION

*W*hat will you do to cut down the busyness of your life? What distractions will you eliminate?

TODAY'S WISDOM

*W*e have been seeking everywhere for [rest] but where there is a prospect of finding it; and that is within ourselves, in a meek and lowly disposition of heart.

LAURENCE STERNE

Start Each Day
with God

⁐⁑⁐

Because He has inclined His ear to me,
therefore I shall call upon Him as long as I live.
PSALM 116:2

*W*HO HAS TIME TO START EACH DAY WITH GOD?" you say. "I'm
so busy. My 'To Do' list is already too long. If I spend any
more time with one more thing I'll get behind!" Priority, priority, priority! We need to figure out what's most important
in life.

By the time we've reached this stage in our lives, we should
have our priorities lined out. One of the great things about the
empty-nest years is that we have more time just for ourselves.
But even though we have more free time, we must still select
the important issues to follow.

I've designed part of my walk-in closet as a "prayer closet."
That's my favorite spot to get away from everyone and all the
distractions. I can't hear the phone ring or be interrupted by
a solicitor ringing the doorbell. It's just me and the Lord.
Beside my special Victorian slipper chair, which my Bob gave
to me for my birthday, I have a wicker basket full of all my
prayer tools: a Bible, a devotional book, Kleenex, my prayer

journal, a packet of notecards, a pen. I do a lot of correspondence in this quiet corner.

I first started by allotting 15 minutes to spend with God, but now that often goes to an hour. I pray, I listen, I respond to God. When I exit my closet, I'm ready for the day's events. I feel refreshed, challenged, at peace, and ready to meet the world.

Paul writes in Galatians 5:22-23 nine "fruit of the Spirit" that come from spending time with God. They are: love, joy, peace, patience, kindness, goodness, faithfulness, gentleness, self-control. Think about each item in that list. Which of us doesn't need a touch of these in our lives?

A basic question we as grandparents must ask ourselves is, Are we doing what's important in our day—or only what is urgent? I've found that people do what they want to do. All of us make choices, and when we don't make time for the most important relationship in our lives, we are probably not making the best choices.

God greatly desires to spend time alone with you. After all, you are His child. He created you. He loves you. He gave His only Son for your salvation. Your heavenly Father wants you to know Him. He wants to meet with you daily. How can you say no to such an opportunity?

The times and places where you meet God will vary, but the fact that you meet alone with Him each day should be a constant in your life. Grandparents need all the spiritual strength they can get. To keep up with the energy and movement of our kids...and their kids!...we need to possess the nine elements of the fruit of the Spirit.

❧❧❧

PRAYER

*F*ather God, may I never forget to call on You in every situation. I want to meet with You every day of my life and bring before You my adoration, confession, thanksgiving, and supplications. Thank You for being willing to be within the sound of my voice and only a thought's distance away. Amen.

ACTION

*R*ead Galatians 5:22-23 and ponder the nine fruit of the Spirit. Select an area that you need to work on for this week.

TODAY'S WISDOM

The Difference

I got up early one morning and rushed into the day;
I had so much to accomplish that I didn't have time to pray.

Problems just tumbled about me, and heavier came each task.
"Why doesn't God help me?" I wondered. He answered, "You didn't ask."

I wanted to see joy and beauty, but the day toiled on, gray and bleak;
I wondered why God didn't show me. He said, "But you didn't seek."

I tried to come into God's presence; I used all my keys at the lock.
God gently and lovingly chided, "My child, you didn't knock."

I woke up early this morning, and paused before entering the day;
I had so much to accomplish that I had to take time to pray.

GRACE L. NAESSNES

Who Moved Away?

❧❧

Behold, like the clay in the potter's hand,
so are you in My hand.

JEREMIAH 18:6

*W*HEN BRAD, MY SON, WAS IN elementary school, the teacher asked the class to shape clay into something. Molded and shaped with his small hands, this red dinosaur-type thing Brad proudly brought home is still on my bookshelf today. Now his children are able to view this prized exhibit of their father's artistry.

Later, in high school, Brad enrolled in a ceramics class. His first pieces were crooked and misshaped, but as time went on he made some pieces of carefully crafted art—vases, pots, pitchers, and various other types of pottery. Many pieces of clay he threw on the pottery wheel, however, took a different direction than he intended. Brad would work and work to reshape the clay. Sometimes he would have to start over, working and working to make it exactly the way he wanted it to be.

With each one of us, God has "taken a handful of clay" to make us exactly who He wants us to be. He is the Master Potter, and we are the vessels in His hands. As He shapes us on His potter's wheel, He works on the inside and the outside. He says, "I am with you. I am the Lord of your life, and I will build within you a strong foundation based on My Word."

The Master Potter also uses the circumstances of life to shape us. But when a child dies, we lose our jobs, fire destroys our homes, finances dissolve, marriages fall apart, or our children or grandchildren rebel, the Potter can seem far away. We may feel forgotten by God, so we pull away from Him because He "let us down." Then, as time passes, God seems even more silent and distant. It seems like the Potter's work is put on hold. But God said, "I will not fail you or forsake you" (Joshua 1:5).

When we feel far from God, we need to remember that He didn't put us on a shelf. *We* are the ones who moved away. He's ready to continue molding us into the people He intents us to be.

In pottery the clay is baked at a very high temperature to set the clay so the vessel won't leak. Sometimes the true beauty of the clay and any glaze comes out only after the firing. The fires of life can do the same for our faith and our character. When we go through trials, we can rest in the knowledge that the Master Potter is at work in our lives.

PRAYER

*F*ather God, help me to trust You more each day as I give back what belongs to You. Give me patience to accept the design You have for my life. Amen.

ACTION

*G*ive back to God what you have taken away from
Him because you didn't feel you could trust Him—
your family, your home, your children, your grandchildren, your looks, and your finances.

TODAY'S WISDOM

I have no yesterdays,
Time took them away;
Tomorrow may not be—
But I have today.

PEARL YEADON MCGINNIS

Making a House into a Home

❧❧❧

This is now bone of my bones, and flesh of my flesh; she shall
be called Woman, because she was taken out of man.

GENESIS 2:23

*I*N OUR SCRIPTURE READING TODAY, we are reminded that God
Himself established the family. Today's secular world is trying
its hardest to downgrade the family as an institution, but we
know God will not abandon the good work He has begun in
the family structure He created (Philippians 1:6).

The Bible is very clear in its teaching that woman was created for man; she is to be his helpmate. The Scripture also
clearly teaches that man and woman are designed for each
other. These are key elements in God's plan for His people. Do
you have a plan for your family? Have you and your mate
taken time to determine what values you want to instill in
your children and grandchildren and what guidelines you will
give them as they grow?

Marriage causes a man to leave his mother and father, be
united with his wife, and become one flesh with her. Is this a
description of what happened in your life? Is it also something you are trying to instill in your children's lives as they
take on mates? We are to encourage "leaving and cleaving" as

part of this married couple. The cord has been broken, and we are no longer responsible for them. They, by being married, have taken on new roles—that of spouse and, eventually, the development of their own families. We must be willing to walk that thin line between being a parent and a grandparent. It's no longer the same as it was when we were parenting. We must follow God's plan for having a healthy family. Strong families are important for individuals and for our nation. Lee Iacocca says,

> My father told me that the best way to teach is by example. He certainly showed me what it took to be a good person and a good citizen. As the old joke has it, "No one ever said on his deathbed, I should have spent more time on my business." Throughout my life, the bottom line I've worried about most was that my kids turn out all right.
>
> The only rock I know that stays steady, the only institution I know that works, is the family. I was brought up to believe in it—and I do. Because I think a civilized world can't remain civilized for long if its foundation is built on anything but the family. A city, state, or country can't be any more than the sum of its vital parts—millions of family units. You can't have a country or a city or a state that's worth [anything] unless you govern within yourself in your day-to-day life.
>
> It all starts at home.[1]

PRAYER

*F*ather God, remind me that I'm responsible for the home and what happens inside. Give me the convictions to be brave in my walk with You. I know it will come with a price, but I stand ready to be counted for Your cause. Bless my home. Amen.

ACTION

*M*eet with your spouse and begin to prayerfully design a master plan for your family.

TODAY'S WISDOM

*T*he Bible does not say very much about homes; it says a great deal about the things that make them. It speaks about life and love and joy and peace and rest. If we get a house and put these into it, we shall have secured a home.

JOHN HENRY JOWETT

Spirit Lifters

♥ Create a "friendship party," where you invite your friends, serve a light lunch, tea, and dessert. I love to do this in the spring.

♥ Keep a list of blessings in your life. Go over the list each morning, and remember that you have reason to celebrate every day.

♥ If there are small children in your life, think of ways to make your life "child friendly" as well as childproof. Tuck a basket of children's books and toys in a corner and toss a few throw pillows beside it to make a welcoming place to play.

♥ Design a "love shelf" in your home to display those little creative gifts from friends and family that mean so much.

❦

Don't Forsake Me

❧❧❧

And now that I am old and gray, don't forsake me.
Give me time to tell this new generation (and
their children too) about all your mighty miracles.
PSALM 71:18 TLB

W E'RE IN A SEASON OF LIFE THAT CHALLENGES what we do with
our days because time is getting shorter. In today's verse, the
psalmist pleads for God not to forsake him until he declares
the power of God to the next generation. Wow! What a great
prayer! I guess that's why I do what I do. I want to tell
everyone, starting with my immediate family and branching
out to others, about the power and the might of God.

One of my favorite passages of Scripture gives me a vision
of how I can touch the next generation. It's found in Titus
2:3-5 NIV: "Likewise, teach the older women to be reverent in
the way they live, not to be slanderers or addicted to much
wine, but to teach what is good. Then they can train the
younger women to love their husbands and children, to be
self-controlled and pure." If only we could grasp the vastness
of these words. Don't wait until you are old and gray-haired.
Begin today![2]

❧❧❧

PRAYER

Father God, I need You. Take control of my life. Make me the kind of person You want me to be. Amen.

ACTION

Decide to be a grandparent for God. Share the gospel with those you love.

TODAY'S WISDOM

The closest friends I have made all through life have been people who also grew up close to a loved and loving grandfather and grandmother.

MARGARET MEAD

There Are Friendship Blessings in Gray Hair

⧞⧞⧞

A cord of three strands is not quickly torn apart.

ECCLESIASTES 4:12

ONE OF THE GREAT BLESSINGS of being a grandma is that we have had ample time to develop friendships with our mates and those we have known for 30-plus years.

Unfortunately, even within this time frame, we may not have developed close relations like we would like. And if we aren't the ones who lack friendships, we probably know those who do. Throughout Scripture we are encouraged to nurture friendship in our relationships. We know there is strength in numbers and in unity.

King Solomon, in all his wisdom, told us that friends are great blessings to our family. Hear what he says, as recorded in Ecclesiastes, chapter 4:

- Two are better than one because they have good return for their labor (verse 9).
- Woe to the one who falls when there is not another to lift him up (verse 10).
- If two lie down together they keep warm (verse 11).

- Two can resist [one who tries to overpower them] (verse 12a).
- A cord of three strands is not quickly torn apart (verse 12b).

As maturing adults, are we working on relationships that build these kinds of blessings? We are never too old to make new and lasting friendships! Begin at home with your family members. Unity should be our goal as husband/wife, parent/child, sibling/sibling, grandparent/child, and grandparent/grandchild. If you haven't already started, begin to develop those traits that have eternal worth, not the temporal traits that live for the moment. Yes, it takes work to have and maintain friends, but the blessings are certainly worth the effort!

In Ecclesiastes 4:8, Solomon asks one of the most basic questions of life: "For whom am I laboring and depriving myself of pleasure?" Is it all for vanity? Does it have any redeeming value to you and your family? If not, do something about it! That's why I love to endorse grandparenting! It gives all the joy that one could ever ask for. Sharing friendship and love with the next generation is one of the blessings God gives us.

ॐ

PRAYER

*F*ather God, in my heart and soul I want my family
to be a blessing to me, and I, likewise, want to be a
blessing to them. At times life seems to be in vain.

Bring to mind those traits that are so important for friendships. I do want to be counted as a friend to those around me. Let me be a discerning person when it comes to doing my best for the people You have placed in my life. Let me major on major issues and minor on minor issues. Amen.

ACTION

Ask yourself this basic question: For whom am I laboring and depriving myself of pleasure?

TODAY'S WISDOM

Lord, make me an instrument of Thy peace; where there is hatred, let me sow love; where there is injury, pardon; where there is doubt, faith; where there is despair, hope; where there is darkness, light; where there is sadness, joy.

ST. FRANCIS OF ASSISI

The Power
of Gentleness

❧❧❧

*We proved to be gentle among you, as a nursing mother
tenderly cares for her own children.*

1 THESSALONIANS 2:7

GRANDPARENTS ARE AT A STAGE in their lives where they can be
gentle giants. My Bob's grandfather on his father's side of the
family was a very tough disciplinarian when raising Bob's dad
and his five siblings. However, to Bob and his brothers, he was
very gentle. He plowed behind a team of mules on his West
Texas cotton farm until his mid-seventies. When Bob was
around "Papa," he felt protected and comforted by his presence.

One of the great compliments we can receive is that of
being gentle. Paul, Silvanus, and Timothy were compassionate,
spiritual mentors to the Thessalonica church. These were very
rugged macho men who were not afraid to be known as gentle
warriors. Although they exhibited these gentle traits, they also
exhorted, confronted, and admonished the Thessalonians as a
father does to his children (1 Thessalonians 2:11).

While raising our children, my Bob considered himself a
very strict father. However, recently our daughter, Jenny, commented that she considered her father to be very gentle. That
was a surprise—and at the same time a compliment. As adults

we need gentleness when we teach our children and grandchildren how to reflect God's glory. In the lives of these children we can rejoice when we see where they are spiritually. A prominent pastor once stated, "Those who minister the gospel should be gentle, tender and affectionate...what is wrong we should oppose, but it should be in the kindest manner toward those who do wrong."

As we lead with gentleness, we will see those around us gladly respond to our leadership. What a wonderful legacy to leave to our children and grandchildren—"Grammy" was such a gentle person.

ꔛ

PRAYER

*F*ather God, may I be tough when I need to, but let it be tempered by a gentle spirit. I want gentleness to be my hallmark. Amen.

ACTION

*L*et's apply gentleness toward others today and note the power in that tenderness.

TODAY'S WISDOM

Gentleness is love in society....It is that cordiality of aspect and that soul of speech, which assure that kind and earnest hearts may still be met with here below. It is that quiet influence, which, like the scented flame of an alabaster lamp, fills many a home with light and warmth and fragrance altogether. It is the carpet, soft and deep, which, whilst it diffuses a look of ample comfort, deadens many a creaking sound. It is the curtain, which from many a beloved form wards off at once the summer's glow and the winter's wind. It is the pillow on which sickness lays its head and forgets half its misery, and to which death comes in a balmier dream. It is considerateness. It is tenderness of feeling. It is warmth of affection. It is promptitude of sympathy. It is love in all its depths and all its delicacy. It is every thing included in that matchless grace, the gentleness of Christ.

Dr. J. Hamilton

Choose Whom
You Will Serve

❧❧❧

If it is disagreeable in your sight to serve the LORD,
choose for yourselves today whom you will serve: whether the
gods which your fathers served which were beyond the River,
or the gods of the Amorites in whose land you are living;
but as for me and my house, we will serve the LORD.

JOSHUA 24:15

*P*RAYER IS NOT A HARD REQUIREMENT—it is the natural privilege of a person to his or her Creator. To those of us who pray, it is a precious time, for it is the way that God sends down blessings to us and the way that He answers our needs.

Anything that hinders us from prayer is wrong. Nothing during our daily duties is more important than our time in prayer. If at all possible, husbands and wives should pray together. As a family if we are not joined together in prayer, how can we expect to receive all of God's blessings for us? We must seek God's guidance if we are to accomplish our goals in life. And if we don't model a prayer life in our homes, our children...and their children...will grow up indifferent to our faith and, in many cases, they will reject our Christianity. Prayer is also critical to making wise decisions in our lives.

Life is made up of decisions and choices. Much of what we are is a compilation of choices we have made over our lifetimes. If we make bad choices, we usually end up in negative situations. In my experience, successful people usually have a history of making good choices.

In our Scripture verse today, we see that Joshua and the people he led had a big decision to make. Which god would they choose? This is basically the same decision for us. Which god will we choose? The choice we make will determine our eternal destiny! Be like Joshua, and choose the one true God! And then share your faith! Parents and grandparents will be eternally judged by how well they teach their children and grandchildren in the faith. Paul, in Romans 12:2, commands us not to be "conformed to this world, but be transformed by the renewing of your mind, so that you may prove what the will of God is."[3]

❧❧

PRAYER

*F*ather God, You chose me, now I choose You. I truly want to serve You, my Lord and Savior. Help me lead my family in Your ways. Amen.

ACTION

*B*e deliberate in your faith today. Share with your children and grandchildren a time of prayer. If you can't do this in person, send a note or give them a call.

TODAY'S WISDOM

Our Father, who are in heaven, bless the provisions of Thy bounty now set before us, and feed our souls with the bread of life, for Christ's sake. Thou hast again supplied our returning wants. Continue, we pray Thee, to be our God and keeper, supply the wants of the destitute, and fill the earth with Thy glory, for Christ's sake. Amen.

LUTHER'S SMALL CATECHISM

From
Grammy's Kitchen

Sunshine Shake

Amount: 1 or 2 servings (almost 2 cups)

    1. Place the ingredients below in a blender.

       1 medium orange, peeled, chopped
       1 medium banana, peeled, broken into chunks
       ½ cup low-fat plain or vanilla yogurt
       1/16 teaspoon nutmeg
       1/16 teaspoon cinnamon

    2. Cover blender and blend on high speed until mixture is smooth (about 1 minute).

    3. To serve, pour into one large or two smaller glasses.

Orange Frosty

Amount: 3 or 4 servings (about 4 cups)

    1. Place ingredients in a blender in the following order:

       6-oz. can frozen orange juice concentrate, unsweetened
       6-oz. juice can (¾ cup) low-fat milk
       ¼ cup non-instant nonfat dry milk powder
       1 banana, peeled, broken into chunks
       ¼ teaspoon vanilla extract
       ice cubes to fill up blender

2. Cover blender and blend on high speed until ice cubes are completely crushed (about 30 seconds).

3. To serve, fill glasses and drink immediately. This drink does not store well in the refrigerator. Drink slowly! You might want to eat it with a spoon.

Special Tip: Leftover *Orange Frosty* makes yummy Popsicles!

A Household Hint for the Kitchen

A one-dozen-size egg carton fits perfectly in the bottom of a large grocery sack. Then when tea bags, coffee grounds, and wet items are thrown away, the carton absorbs the liquid and prevents the trash bags from dripping on the carpet when carried from the house to outside trash cans.

"Can't You Say It, Grandpa?"

Behold, children are a gift of the LORD.
PSALM 127:3

*D*O YOUR GRANDCHILDREN KNOW you love them? Do they know unconditional acceptance? Are they winners in your eyes? Do they know that? Grandchildren need to know that grandparents really love them. They long to hear us say, "I love you, and I am very proud of you." And they need to know we love them even when they...

- yell and scream in the grocery store,
- have temper tantrums in a restaurant,
- wear strange clothes,
- have funny haircuts and oddly colored hair,
- use vulgar language,
- run away from home,
- do poorly in school,
- run around with questionable friends.

Often children use behaviors such as these to ask, "Do you

33

love me always?" What are your children "hearing" from your reaction?[4]

❦❦❦

PRAYER

*F*ather God, teach me to show my grandchildren that I love them and prod me to tell them with words too. Amen.

ACTION

*W*rite a note to each of your grandchildren—whatever their ages—and let them know how much you love them. Be specific about a few things you love about them.

TODAY'S WISDOM

*T*wo stonecutters were asked what they were doing. The first one said, "I'm cutting this stone into blocks." The second replied, "I'm on a team that's building a cathedral."

A Friend
Is Waiting

❧

*Surely goodness and lovingkindness will follow me
all the days of my life, and I will
dwell in the house of the LORD forever.*

PSALM 23:6

WHAT A GREAT TRUTH TO KNOW that God actually loves and cares for me! I had a difficult time realizing that God would have died on the cross just for me and my sins. I don't want Jesus to have to wait for my stubbornness before I relinquish control of my life and tell Him that I love Him too.

Jesus must have a lot of patience to wait for us. I'm sure He longs and cries for our repentance, but we just go along living our own selfish lives, doing our own thing—whatever that might be.

Have you already made a decision to accept the claims of Jesus as your Savior? I hope so! One of the Barnes' mottoes is: "A foolish man does in his old age what a wise man does in his youth." Don't put off until it's too late to make that decision. Some verses of Scripture that might be of help in your decision-making process are:

- John 3:16
- John 17:3

- Romans 3:23
- Romans 6:23
- Romans 5:8
- John 14:6
- 1 Corinthians 15:3-6
- Ephesians 2:8-9
- John 3:1-8
- Revelation 3:20

PRAYER

*Y*ou can receive Jesus right now by faith through this suggested prayer:

> Lord Jesus, I want to know You personally. Thank You for dying on the cross for my sins. I open the door of my life and receive You as my Savior and Lord. Thank You for forgiving my sins and giving me eternal life. Take control of the throne of my life. Make me the kind of person You want me to be. Amen.[5]

ACTION

*S*hare this decision with your mate.

TODAY'S WISDOM

*D*ear Friend:

I just had to send a note to tell you how much I love you and care about you. I saw you yesterday as you were walking with your friends. I waited all day hoping you would want to talk with me also. As evening drew near, I gave you a sunset to close your day and a cool breeze to rest you. And I waited. But you never came. It hurt me, but I still love you because I am your friend.

I saw you fall asleep last night and I longed to touch your brow. So I spilled moonlight on your pillow and your face. Again I waited, wanting to rush down so we could talk. I have so many gifts for you. But you awakened late the next day and rushed back to work. My tears were in the rain.

Today you looked so sad, so all alone. It makes my heart ache because I understand. My friends let me down and hurt me so many times too. But I love you. Oh, if you would only listen to me. I really love you. I try to tell you in the blue sky and in the quiet green grass. I whisper it in the leaves on the trees and breathe it in the colors of the flowers. I shout it to you in the mountain streams and give the birds love songs to sing. I clothe you with warm sunshine and perfume the air with nature's scents. My love for you is deeper than the oceans and bigger than the biggest want or need in your heart.

If you only knew how much I want to help you. I want you to meet my Father. He wants to help you too. My Father is that way, you know. Just call me, ask me, talk with me. I have so much to share with you. Yet I won't hassle you. I'll wait because I love you.

Your Friend,
Jesus[6]

A Life Well Lived

☙❧

*The Christian home is the master's workshop
where the process of character-molding is silently,
lovingly, faithfully and successfully carried on.*
RICHARD M. MILNES

*A*s WE GRANDPARENTS MATURE IN AGE, we become aware of how effective our modeling has been with our children and grandchildren. Oftentimes they will share with us stories and memories that we didn't think were so significant in our lives, but they had an enormous impact on those around us. Such was the life of Bob Marrero. The following eulogy was read by his daughter, Cookie Strickland, at his funeral service on March 16, 2001.

☙❧

Before there was a James Dobson or a Bill McCartney... there was Bob Marrero. Before "just do it" was a million-dollar campaign slogan...he was...just doing it. Before Promise Keepers was a movement, it was a lifestyle for him. And before the experts were debating about whether children needed "quality" time or "quantity" time, he was giving his kids both.

To be called upon to describe the 83 years of the life of the man I call "Daddy" is perhaps one of the hardest things I've ever had to do. And yet, it is also my highest honor. Because although I did not choose my dad, if I could have, I would have. If God had taken me by the hand before I was born and shown me every possible choice for a father that I could have had, I would have picked the one He gave me.

Not everyone can say that. My father could not say that. His father was institutionalized in 1929, and from that day on, my dad became the man of his household. At age 11 he was called upon to care for his mother, provide for the family, and still continue his schooling. If I have any regrets, it is that I do not know more about that time in my dad's life. What I do know is that even though his childhood was racked with difficulty and trials, it affected him only for good. My father never blamed his father for anything. He simply rose above the circumstances, trusted deeply in God's bigger plan, and lived his life in honor.

I believe with all my heart that the person I am today is deeply wrapped up in the man my father was and the home he provided for me. I've heard it said that it is the mother that sets the tone for the family. You know, "If mama ain't happy, nobody's happy." But I have come to disagree with that. I truly believe that it is the demeanor and attitude of the dad that largely determines what a home will be like. In my case, it could not have been better. He didn't have the parenting manuals; he didn't read the "how to" books; he just loved us beyond compare and gave us everything of himself.

This man taught me to fish and then spent time with me doing it. He taught me to play baseball by taking his glove with me into the street after supper. He taught me to laugh by making every meal an experience with his quick humor and dry wit. He taught me to care for my fellow man as I watched him late into the evening pull his pants on over his pajamas and go out into the night to take someone a part for his car. He taught me to be a lady because he treated me like one. He taught me to make my own decisions by allowing me to fail. He taught me the value of a dollar by showing me that an honest day's work by the sweat of your brow was something to find pride in and that saving your money was an okay thing to do. He told me I was important in his life because *never* was he too busy to take care of anything I asked of him. He took me to school every day. I *knew* I could always count on Daddy. He was true to his word. And most of all he taught me to love Jesus with all my heart because that is what he did so easily.

It was never difficult for me to love my heavenly Father because of the deep similarity of my earthly father to Him. I never *ever* wanted to disappoint my dad. Why would I ever want to rebel against God if He was even better than Daddy? It made no sense to me, so I never did.

I am proud to be from a blue-collar home. I am proud to be the daughter of a parts manager. When I went to see him at his office, I believed he was the most important man on the planet. He showed me that the true test of character comes in how you live, not in what you do. I am so very, very blessed to have shared this life with Bob Marrero.

When I was a little girl, my daddy was everything. Scripture says that there are three things the Lord requires of us: "to do justice, to love mercy and to walk humbly with our God." If I had to summarize his life, this would be it. I have never known a more humble man, and because of that, he was truly a *great* man. He led me to a deep faith in my heavenly Father that will carry me into eternity. He loved me beyond compare. We all have one shot. He took it—and did it well. His truly was *a life well lived.*[7]

ꔙꔙ

PRAYER

*F*ather God, what a wonderful example of parent-
hood and Christianity. May I be so blessed by having
such an impact on my children and grandchildren.
May all who read this eulogy be encouraged to live a
life worth living. Amen.

ACTION

*P*urchase your grandchild a book. Record yourself
reading to him/her. He can play the tape over and
over, listening to Grammy.

TODAY'S WISDOM

I expect to pass through the world but once. Any
good therefore that I can do, or any kindness or abilities that I can show to any fellow creature, let me do
it now. Let me not defer or neglect it, for I shall not
pass this way again.

WILLIAM PENN

Spirit Lifters

♥ Next time you make buttered toast, sprinkle on some cinnamon and sugar. An old idea, but when was the last time you did it?

♥ Rearrange your bedroom furniture so that the first thing you see as you enter the room is the bed. Place a small vase of flowers on each side of the bed.

♥ Try setting aside a "quiet corner" at home with books, comfortable cushions, some warm lighting. Have the family agree to make stillness a priority when they use this area.

♥ Try taking your hospitality on the road. Fill a basket with food, and take it to someone who needs encouragement.

The Messes in Life
Are a Blessing

❧❧❧

But if anyone does not provide for his own,
and especially for those of his household,
he has denied the faith, and is worse than an unbeliever.

1 TIMOTHY 5:8

*I*N AMERICA WE ARE A NATION of convenience. We like it the way
we like it—and please hurry, I want it now! Preparations are
a lot more fun than cleanups. Messes are not fun. That's why
paper goods are so popular. All you have to do is throw them
away. No need for soap and water, dishwashers, or drying
towels. Everything goes into the trash can.

"Billy, would you please help with the dishes tonight? I've
had such a hard day at work, and I just don't have the energy
to do one more thing." Billy's reply is like that of many
teenagers, "But Mom, I wasn't the only one to make the mess.
The rest of the family needs to help out too. I just hate dirty
dishes. Why can't we use paper plates?"

Does this conversation sound familiar to you? Who likes
the mess that goes with a meal? Wouldn't it be great if
somehow the dishes took care of themselves? But of course
they don't; messes need attention.

Much of life is how we look at things. Are we positive or
are we negative? Is our glass half-full or half-empty?

Let's see if we can turn the messes of our lives into blessings. In order for us to have dirty dishes, it means we have eaten food, and in most cases more food than we need. We have leftovers, which means we had plenty of food. Let's thank God for the abundance rather than the mess it makes. Let's go a step further and teach our family members to thank God for giving us enough food so we can have dirty dishes. And how many of our other messes are evidence that God has given us abundance?

- How about clothes that need washing and ironing?
- Lawns that need to be mowed?
- Beds that need to be made?
- Carpets that need vacuuming?
- A refrigerator that needs cleaning?
- A school that we need to walk to?
- A job that we need to drive to?
- A home that needs painting?
- A television that needs repairs?

As wise grandparents, we have the opportunity to share with our grandchildren how messes can be a blessing. This would be a great opportunity to point out to them that only because of God's abundances in our lives are we able to have messes.[8]

PRAYER

*F*ather God, thank You for reminding me that my messes are really a sign of abundance and that You are the one who so richly gives. Thank You for all that You provide. Amen.

ACTION

*A*s a family, discuss the messes of your lives. What are the hidden blessings?

TODAY'S WISDOM

*H*ow little do my countrymen know what precious blessings they are in possession of, and which no other people on earth enjoy.

THOMAS JEFFERSON

Grandparents Need
to Be Friends

❧❧❧

A friend loves at all times.
PROVERBS 17:17

THERE IS NO GREATER SIGHT OR JOY than to see two grandparents walking on the beach arm in arm. To us it reflects the truth that love and friendship can endure over time. In our youth-oriented culture, people often believe that love and friendship are only for the young. Somehow older folks aren't supposed to be friends and to love each other.

Genesis 2:18-23 is a beautiful picture of how God created not only the first woman and wife, but also man's (Adam's) first friend. The Lord said, "It is not good for the man to be alone. I will make him a helper suitable for him" (verse 18). A wife is indeed her husband's friend. Through the years Bob's and my love for each other has grown, and we have become each other's best friend. This passage from Genesis suggests that is exactly what God intends for a married couple.

One of the great models we have for our children and grandchildren is that Papa and Grammy truly love each other and express affection for their friendship. The children and grandchildren love to overhear the words of affection that are expressed and see manners and courtesies we extend to each other. Your love for your partner gives them hope for their marriages and the grandchildren's future desires to be married. Our granddaughter Christine often says, "I want to marry a man just like Papa." What a thrill to realize that our love has had some effect on another person's life.

Alan Toy McGinnis, in his book *The Friendship Factor,* gives a good description of what a friend is: "And what is a friend? Many things....A friend is someone you are comfortable with, someone whose company you prefer. A friend is someone you can count on—not only for support, but for honesty...who senses my struggle, who shares my lows as well as my highs."[9] In this friendship, nothing is hidden. Friendship is built on trust, and friendship takes time to grow and develop. What better context for this kind of friendship to grow than from your marriage!

How does your marriage measure up against this description? If you and your husband don't yet share this kind of friendship, don't wait for him to reach out. Take the initial step and see how he responds. If you have tried before and not been well received, ask God to guide and bless your efforts and then risk reaching out again.

✥✥✥

PRAYER

Father God, I thank You for the love and friendship You have kindled between my husband and me. The older we get the deeper our love and friendship grows. Your Word has been our guiding light. Amen.

ACTION

*W*rite your spouse a note expressing how much you enjoy him as a friend.

TODAY'S WISDOM

*S*o long as we love, we serve; so long as we are loved by others, I should say that we are almost indispensable; and no man is useless while he has a friend.

ROBERT LOUIS STEVENSON

A Lesson in Jelly Beans

❧❧❧

For God so loved the world,
that He gave His only begotten Son,
that whoever believes in Him shall not perish,
but have eternal life.

JOHN 3:16

As GRANDPARENTS, WE ARE ALWAYS looking to teach a "life lesson." A "life lesson" is something that once taught is never forgotten. As teachers, we must survey all the events that go on around us and sift out the chaff from the wheat. I have found that my grandchildren love jelly beans. Ex-President Ronald Reagan advanced the popularity of jelly beans when he was in office. He always had a jar of them on his desk. If you visited this fine president, you were offered the opportunity to extend your hand into the jar and bring out a handful of these delightful yummies.

Do you realize that the various colors and flavors have a story? My grandchildren love to hear the jelly beans tale.

Little Jelly Beans

Little jelly beans
Tell a story true
A tale of Father's love
Just for me and you.

49

GREEN is for the waving palms
BLUE for the skies above
BROWN for the soft earth where
People sat hearing of HIS love.

A SPECKLED bean for fish and sand
RED for precious wine
And BLACK is for the sin He washed
From your soul and mine.

PURPLE'S for the sadness of
HIS family and friends,
And WHITE is for the glory of the
Day HE rose again.

Now you've heard the story
You know what each color means
The story of our Father's love
Told by some jelly beans.

So every morning take a bean
They're really very yummy
Something for the soul, you see.
And something for the tummy.[10]

Go to your local candy store and purchase an assortment of jelly beans. Make sure you have one of each of the above. After you have taught your loved ones this "life lesson," they will remember to thank their Lord for the earth and sky, for friends and family, for a family of God that is so big and mighty, for the love and prayers of others. And most of all, for our heavenly Father's love—the love gift of His very own Son, Jesus Christ.

PRAYER

*F*ather God, thank You for the simple reminders of who You are and what You have done. You are a great and awesome God. Help me to remember that always. Amen.

ACTION

*G*o out and teach a "life lesson" to someone.

TODAY'S WISDOM

*W*e have only this moment sparkling like a star in our hand…and melting like a snowflake. Let us use it before it is too late.

MARIE EDITH BEYNON

Two-Fisted Faith

❧❧❧

Whoever does not fall down and worship
shall immediately be cast into
the midst of a furnace of blazing fire.

DANIEL 3:6

*F*ORTUNATELY FOR US WHO LIVE IN the western part of the world, we have not been given this type of ultimatum. We are free to worship any sort of god we want—either our almighty God, a god of another religion, or a make-believe god of materialism.

In Daniel 3, King Nebuchadnezzar wanted his people to bow down before his golden idol or face the consequence of death in a fiery furnace.

The heroes of this passage are three Jews: Shadrach, Meshach, and Abed-nego. They had a choice to make, either to bow down before the king's idol or to be thrown into the hot furnace. To them this wasn't going to be a big decision; they knew without question that they would not bow down before the false idol. Thus they knew well and good that they were to be cast into a furnace that might consume their bodies. The prisoners in Daniel 3:16-17 give a classic answer to the king:

> O Nebuchadnezzar, we do not need to give you an
> answer concerning this matter. If it be so, our God

whom we serve is able to deliver us from the furnace of blazing fire; and He will deliver us out of your hand, O king. But even if He does not, let it be known to you, O king, that we are not going to serve your gods and worship the golden image that you have set up.

You must read the remainder of Daniel 3 to get the Paul Harvey ending—the rest of the story. These three men had two assurances of faith:

- God is able...
- But if He chooses not to...

These are our two alternatives when difficulties face us. We can be assured that God is able to see us through, but if not we will still not worship any other god. As grandparents, we are continually challenged to live a life of faith or to bow down before another false idol. Each day we must decide who we will serve. Our two-fisted faith—our firm belief in God—will see us through any and all situations.

PRAYER

Father God, may my faith be two-fisted when it comes to the demands of life. May I rely upon Your promises for all of life's situations. I know You are able to see me through every situation. Amen.

ACTION

If there are any idols you are bowing down to, be willing to say, "No longer!"

TODAY'S WISDOM

We can rejoice, too, when we run into problems and trials, for we know that they are good for us— they help us learn to endure. And endurance develops strength of character in us, and character strengthens our confident expectation of salvation....

ROMANS 5:3-5 NLT

From Grammy's Kitchen

Boboli Pizza—Shrimp Style

Ingredients

> 1 16-ounce Boboli Italian bread shell
> ½ cup seafood cocktail sauce
> 4 ounces low-fat cheese (mozzarella or cheddar)
> 2 cups cooked shrimp (frozen works well)
> thinly sliced green pepper, onions, mushrooms,
>   and tomatoes

Preparation

> Preheat oven to 450 degrees. Place Boboli on pizza
> pan. Spoon on the cocktail sauce and add cheese.
> Arrange shrimp and vegetables over cheese. Bake
> for 8 to 10 minutes or until cheese is melted.

Serves 8

A Household Hint for the Kitchen

See-through jars and plastic containers are great
for storing kitchen items such as tea bags, sugar,
flour, beans, noodles, rice, oatmeal, popcorn,
cookies, and raisins. They keep them fresh and
easy to spot.

There Are
Home Rules in Life

❧❧❧

You shall teach them diligently to your sons.
DEUTERONOMY 6:7

*I*N OUR SCRIPTURE PASSAGE TODAY God outlines the responsibility that we have as parents to teach our children and grandchildren at home and elsewhere. So important were the commands of the Lord that Moses directed us to do everything possible to remember God's instructions and to incorporate them into everyday life. And home is the perfect venue for reaching hearts:

> Home is the one place in all this world where hearts are sure of each other. It is the place of confidence. It is the place where we tear off that mask of guarded and suspicious coldness which the world forces us to wear in self-defense, and where we pour out the unreserved communications of full and confiding hearts. It is the spot where expressions of tenderness gush out without any sensation of awkwardness and without any dread of ridicule.[11]

The spiritual education of the children is primarily the responsibility of the parents, but we as grandparents can do a lot to reinforce these principles when our grandchildren come to visit us. The teaching should take place daily through the example of the parents *and* grandparents. The importance of this command is seen by the extent to which parents were to go in order to teach their children:

> The LORD is our God, the LORD is one! You shall love the LORD your God with all your heart and with all your soul and with all your might. These words...shall be on your heart. You shall teach them diligently to your sons and shall talk of them when you sit in your house and when you walk by the way and when you lie down and when you rise up (Deuteronomy 6:4-7).

This was more than simply teaching the facts of the law; God's ways were to be demonstrated in a lifestyle woven into the tapestry of faith. Creativity is essential in teaching the precepts of God while we are involved in the mundane chores of the household.

That becomes our biggest task today as grandparents—how to teach Christian values and responsibilities in a creative fashion. How can we compete with TV sound bites, Disney mind-sets, computer games, and cell phones? We live in an age of fast-paced technology that throws fast, colorful, and short concentration bites of information to all of us, including our grandchildren. It takes creative grandparenting to stay up with the rat pack. Most often our grandchildren pick up on our walk better than our talk. These youngsters have great discernment in observing how adults live out their lives.

In Deuteronomy 6:7, we find that teaching and learning doesn't always take place in a formal, rigid classroom setting. We are to talk of these principles when we sit in our house, when we walk by the way, when we lie down, and when we rise; that's 24/7! We can integrate biblical truths into everyday settings.

PRAYER

*F*ather God, being a godly grandparent is not easy. Sometimes I just want to go back to the simple life without having to face the awesomeness of helping to raise grandchildren. Restore to my soul the desire to keep on. Please reassure my faith in what I've set out to do—to be obedient to Your commands. Amen.

ACTION

*W*rite out in simple form your home rules. Talk them over with your husband. As grandparents, we need to be in agreement of what we are trying to teach our grandchildren when they come for a visit.

TODAY'S WISDOM

*L*ive neither in the past nor in the future, but let each day's work absorb your entire energies, and satisfy your wildest ambition.

WILLIAM OSLER

Don't Stay
Trapped by the Past

☙❧

Delight yourself in the LORD;
and He will give you the desires of your heart.

PSALM 37:4

*I*F YOU ARE LIKE ME, THERE ARE many things to let go of and not continue to hold on to. As I age and mature (hopefully they go together), I see that I tend to hold on to the past—the memories of the good times when Bob and I were young and happily married, had good jobs and good health, and the children were young. I remember the vacations in the mountains, strolls along the beach, Christmas at Mom and Dad's. Yes, even the memories of the bad times hold me captive. But these old memories can limit us. On occasion our minds so desperately concentrate on the past that we forget to enjoy the thrills of the present or the anticipation of the future.

Bob and I even find ourselves holding on to people. Our insecurities won't let us branch out to meet new friends. In this ever-changing world, it seems more difficult to get to know new people. We need to remind ourselves to risk new relationships instead of focusing solely on our old friends who we have prayed with, laughed with, cried with, vacationed with, and endured transitions with between children and the empty nest. We need to make room for new relationships.

Instead of staying bundled up in the past (even though they were wonderful times), we can pray that God will show us how to let go and move on. We need strength and courage to let go of those past memories so we can experience the fullness of this day and all the tomorrows that God has for us. We pray that God will let us step out in faith to do the things that are ours today and in the future.

Letting go may not be easy, but we know that with God's help we can do it. We can let Him work in our lives. As mature adults, we need to be able to live full and abundant lives. We don't have to be put out to pasture. "Delight yourself in the LORD; and He will give you the desires of your heart" (Psalm 37:4).

❧❧❧

PRAYER

*F*ather God, give me the desire to let go of those things that bind me down and keep me from doing Your kingdom's work. Revive me with the energy to let go and move on. May my desire be in Your will for my life. Amen.

ACTION

*W*ith your mate, sit down and plan four objectives for each of you:

- 30-day goals
- 6-month goals
- 1-year goals
- 2-year goals

TODAY'S WISDOM

*F*orgetting what is behind, and straining toward what is ahead, I press on toward the goal to win the prize for which God has called me heavenward in Christ Jesus.

PHILIPPIANS 3:13-14 NIV

Receive All
of God's Blessings

❧❧❧

And if ye walk contrary unto me...
then will I also walk contrary unto you.
LEVITICUS 26:21,24 KJV

*A*ND WHATSOEVER WE ASK, we receive of him, because we keep his commandments" (1 John 3:22 KJV). Any responsible grandparent can tell you that you cannot grant a disobedient child his wishes. If the grandmother does, then the family disintegrates. Sadly there comes a time when the parent or grandparent must insist that if the child is not obedient to rules of the home or does not listen to wisdom of the adult, then the child will have to go somewhere else.

God acts toward us as we act toward our wayward child. It's not that He doesn't love us, but He responds with "tough love" because He loves us so much. The child or grandchild is still a member of the family, but he will not receive the many blessings afforded him because he was disobedient to wisdom and truth.

I am amazed when I meet individuals who don't look or act like Christians, but in conversation they share that they attended church when they were younger and accepted Jesus as their personal Savior. Their present lives certainly don't reflect those early childhood decisions, yet they still classify themselves as Christians. God is longing for them to return to His way. He wants them—and each of us—to share in His great blessings—all of them!

PRAYER

*F*ather God, if I'm going to be identified with You, then I should be obedient to who You are. I don't want to stand before You at judgment day and hear You say, "Depart from Me. I never knew you." Amen.

ACTION

*S*tand up for God today. Stand as God's light in the world's darkness. Let your grandchild know of your faith.[12]

TODAY'S WISDOM

*Y*et ye have forsaken me, and served other gods: wherefore I will deliver you no more. Go and cry unto the gods which ye have chosen.

JUDGES 10:13-14 KJV

SPIRIT LIFTERS

♥ Fresh flowers are such an inexpensive way of saying welcome. You don't need a whole dozen from the florist. A small bunch from the supermarket, or a flower from your garden in an appropriate vase makes a warm statement.

♥ During the fall, go out to a local farm and pick pumpkins for centerpieces, yard decorations, and of course pumpkin pie! Better yet, plant pumpkin seeds in July for a fall harvest.

♥ Take a hint from a great-grandmother: Dab a bit of vanilla behind your ears for a tasty fragrance.

♥ Your front door will always say welcome with a May basket, a fall arrangement of Indian corn, or a green wreath for Christmas.

The Same
but Different

❦❧

*Here's my advice: Make sure your
children and grandchildren know you love them.*

Barbara Bush

$\mathcal{A}$s we look at today's youth, we might jump to the conclusion that they are so very different from our days. However,
I've learned over the years that every generation is basically the
same…only different.

Parents are so close to the trees they can't see the forest.
They are so close to the children, they aren't able to step back
and see that they are much like their parents. Sure their hair
may be a different color or a different length, but other than
the current fashions, they are not much different inside from
mom and dad.

This is where grandparents play a big role. We are able to
step back, become more objective, and give a better perspective on the situation. The grandparent has lived long enough
to have seen it all. We have seen the good and the bad. We
have seen styles and fashions come and go. We too thought
our children were, at times, irresponsible, strange, and out-to-
lunch. We have experienced the change from impossible to the

possible. Generation after generation has evolved into very capable adults who are now the parents of their own rascals.

As grandparents, we have observed and know that the more children change, the more they remain the same. So we can encourage our children about their children. Remind your kids that their children have the same desires that they had at their age. Sure the kids' lives may be framed differently than your adult children's when they were children, but help your kids continue to love their kids through the process of becoming adults.

PRAYER

*F*ather God, let me be a positive influence upon my children and their children's development into responsible adults and positive contributors to society. Let them know that I love them. Amen.

ACTION

*B*e an encouragement to your grandchildren's parents today. Make contact in some fashion.

TODAY'S WISDOM

*L*et your grandchildren know through words and deeds, that the bond of affection which attaches the two of you to one another can never be broken.

ARTHUR KORNHABER

A One-Penny
Wedding Dress

❧❧❧

But seek first His kingdom and His righteousness,
and all these things will be added to you.
MATTHEW 6:33

WHAT ARE "ALL THESE THINGS" in Matthew 6:33? Could it possibly be a wedding dress? We have some dear friends who live in Arizona who are very future-oriented by their high school daughter's someday wedding. They knew it would be a long time in the future, but why procrastinate on their plan?

Their plan was very simple—they and a few of their friends would save their pennies for buying their daughter's future wedding dress. Whoever heard of purchasing an expensive wedding dress for a penny? People won't even stop to pick up a lost penny on the sidewalk. How can a penny buy a wedding dress?

You can't believe what has happened! Over the years, some friends have gotten behind this endeavor and faithfully set aside all those good-for-nothing pennies. We have helped roll these coins into their paper wrappers and store them away in a secret hiding place in the kitchen pantry. Little pennies added together take up a lot of space and are very heavy.

This spring their daughter and future son-in-law announced that they were to be married in January. At last the big day is approaching! Her parents have big plans for these pennies. This huge load will be loaded into a wheel barrow, rolled into the bank, with a local photographer and newspaper writer standing by to write up this special-interest story.

The last approximate calculation is there are at least $1,000 worth of pennies to be deposited in the daughter's bank account. You really can buy a wedding dress for pennies!

ᔓᔕ

PRAYER

Father God, thank You for adding "all these things" into our passage for today. You truly are a God of little things. We thank You for all the friends who made the wedding-dress dream come true. Amen.

ACTION

Begin saving pennies for your granddaughter's future wedding gown or grandson's tux.

TODAY'S WISDOM

It's good to have money and the things that money can buy, but it's good, too, to check up once in a while and make sure that you haven't lost the things that money can't buy.

GEORGE HORACE LORIMER

Contentment
Brings Joy to Life

ഏൠഏ

I have learned to be content
in whatever circumstances I am.

PHILIPPIANS 4:11

ONE OF THE BARNES' FAMILY MOTTOES IS, "If you're not content with what you have, you'll never be content with what you want." We meet many people who are always looking toward the future—the next paycheck, the next home, the next church, the next month, the next school, and in some cases, the next marriage partner. We are a country characterized by discontent. Do you find yourself being drawn into this mind-set?

A bishop of the early church who was a remarkable example of contentment was asked his secret. The old man replied, "It consists in nothing more than making a right use of my eyes. In whatever circumstance I am, I first of all look up to heaven and remember that my principal business here is to get there. I then look down upon the earth, and remember how small a place I shall occupy in it when I die and am buried. I then look abroad in the world and observe what multitudes there are who are in all respects more unhappy than myself. Thus I learn where true happiness is placed, where all our cares must end, and what little reason I have to complain.[13]

Conditions and situations will never be perfect; if we wait for perfection to be content, we will never be happy. Possessions do not bring us contentment. That only comes about when we focus upon why we are here on earth and then begin to live out our true, godly purpose.

As grandparents, our lives race before us. If we are not careful, we can become discontent with what our lives have or haven't been. We can lose heart and even take on an air of negativity. We must guard our hearts to prevent that from happening. Satan would love to take our joy away. He would take great pride in having our spiritual walk come to a slide over an attitude of discontent.

Stay strong and firm in your faith. In Scripture, Paul tells us to be content in all circumstances. Your response to conditions of life will determine your attitude toward contentment. Rejoice in whatever status you find yourself.

శ్రీఏ

PRAYER

*F*ather God, thanks for encouraging me to be content in my circumstances. I want to live for today. Take away my pursuit of tomorrow because I know You will take care of me. I truly want to thank You for all of my blessings. Your grace is sufficient for my happiness of life. Amen.

ACTION

*I*nstead of being discontent with your station in life, start praising God for where you are.

TODAY'S WISDOM

*T*rue contentment is a real, even an active, virtue—not only affirmative but creative. It is the power of getting out of any situation all there is in it.

G.K. CHESTERTON

The Art of
Good Teaching

*These words, which I am commanding
you today, shall be on your heart. You shall
teach them diligently to your sons.*
DEUTERONOMY 6:6-7

ONE OF OUR GOALS AS GRANDPARENTS is to bring out the very
best in our grandchildren. There are many techniques out
there that tell you how to be good parents. Some are worthwhile and some will be short-lived because they don't have
solid values behind them. In order for techniques to work,
they must be part of your belief system. Business and education constantly look into new areas of research to find out
what makes good managers and teachers. The common strand
for success in both of these areas is to have a genuine caring
attitude for the people they are responsible for. That is true of
grandparenting too. To be effective, you must show your
grandchildren that you really care for them—not just in words
but also in action. Children are continually asking in their
music, friends, clothes, and grades, "Do you really love me?"

As grandparents we want to know how to carry out this
genuine caring. Here are ten qualities that exhibit good grandparenting:

• *Really listen.* This means turn off the radio or TV

and put down the newspaper or magazine so that you can give 100 percent of your attention to your conversation. Tell the other members of the family that you are not to be disturbed unless for a major emergency. Be like one grandparent who said, "I hear not only with my ears, but with my eyes and my guts. I don't want to miss anything, either verbally or nonverbally."

- *Take an interest in your grandchildren as people.* Be interested in them as people, and not only as your grandchildren. Ask them questions: How did school go? How's Mary? How's football? How's church? How's your stomachache? Care about them.

- *Be clear in your expectations.* Tell your grandchildren what you expect, and then give them freedom to do it. Each grandchild may do things differently, based upon his or her temperament. Some grandchildren do things with little flair while others do things with great flair.

- *Be willing to transmit your knowledge to your grandchildren eagerly.* Take time to explain, demonstrate, and answer their questions—even if they seem simple to you. Give your grandkids time when you're walking, when you lie down, and when you get up.

- *Reinforce positive behaviors and discourage unacceptable performance.* Compliment good work by making your grandchildren know what specifically is being praised. This way you are more likely to get repeat performances. Conversely, by being specific about what needs to be improved, you teach them to perform at a higher level than they normally do.

- *Trust your grandchildren to fulfill their promises.* Train them how to keep their word. One of my favorite mottoes is, "Just do what you say you are going to do." We are to keep our word by keeping our appointments, calling back when we say we will, and turning in homework assignments on time. Let your grandchildren work out the details by themselves.

- *Be flexible and remain open to good ideas.* Admit when you are wrong, and be willing to change your mind when the evidence shows you are wrong. Don't think you have all the answers. Let answers to the questions come from all members of the family.

- *Have a good sense of humor.* Humor and enthusiasm are infectious and create a friendly, productive atmosphere. Learn to laugh at yourself. It's more fun to be in a family that can laugh with each other and not at each other.

- *Challenge and set standards that raise the standards.* Search for excellence, not perfection. Lift the members of the family to a notch higher than they would reach by themselves.

- *Stay in control of the family unit.* Even if things go astray, the family members will stay loyal and supportive of its leadership if the leaders are in control. That means in language, body motions, attitudes, temperament, and balance. We as parents and grandparents must exhibit the highest standards for ourselves. We can't ask our children and grandchildren to go beyond a standard that we don't exhibit ourselves.

PRAYER

Father God, give me the strength and endurance to be faithful in my Christian walk. May my spiritual fragrance be a sweet smell. May those around me be inspired by my presence. Amen.

ACTION

The next time your grandchildren come to spend the night, write each of them an uplifting note about them and place it under their pillows. If they don't live close by, mail the notes to their homes.

TODAY'S WISDOM

Knowledge is horizontal. Wisdom is vertical—it comes down from above.

BILLY GRAHAM[14]

Staying on Top of Life

❧❧❧

In all your ways acknowledge Him,
and He will make your paths straight.

PROVERBS 3:6

*A*S A GRANDPARENT, I HAVE REALIZED that I must be organized in my home and personal life if I'm going to stay on top of life. The rhythm of a grandparent is much different than the flow of a parent. I find that I now run in spurts. However, the good side is that there is more down time during these spurts. The negative side is that if I don't consistently attend to details, they slide away and then it takes a bulldozer to get things back together.

Do you have the type of home where nothing seems to get done (particularly in-between these spurts)? You rush around all day never completing any one job, or if you do complete a task, there is a little one behind you pulling and messing everything up. Again. We've all had these experiences, either with our children or grandchildren.

When I was twenty years old, our baby daughter was six months old. We then took in my brother's three children and within a few months I became pregnant with our son. That gave Bob and me five children under five years old. My life was work-work-work—and I never seemed to get anywhere. I was always tired-tired-tired. I was running on a treadmill that never stopped and never moved ahead. I was fragmented, totally confused, and stressed out.

Then one day, during my rushed quiet time with my Lord, I read Proverbs 3:6: "In all your ways acknowledge Him, and He will make your paths straight." I fell to my knees and prayed, "Please, God, direct my path. I acknowledge You to help me, Lord. I'm going to allow You to lead me and not lead myself in my power. I want Your power and direction. Lord, I'm tired. I'm on overload with husband, children, and meals. I have no time left over for me or anyone else. I can't even do any of them justice. Please help me to put it all together and make it work to glorify You. Amen."

The Lord not only heard my prayer that day, but He honored it as well. I began a program that changed my life. I committed 15 minutes per day to my quiet time with the Lord. With baby Brad in hand, I got up earlier each morning. The house was quiet, and my Lord and I talked as I read His Word and prayed.

Next I committed 15 minutes each day to the organization of our home, concentrating on things I never seemed to get done: the silverware drawer, the refrigerator, hall closets, photos, bookshelves, piles of papers. I committed to this for 30 days, and the pattern was set. God was directing my path.

Our home changed dramatically. The cloud of home-making stress lifted, and I had new direction. The Lord redeemed my time with Him. I had more time to plan meals, make new recipes, play with the children, take walks to the park, even catch a nap from time to time.

Looking back now, I can truly understand the meaning of acknowledging God in all my ways. That means looking to Him for help and comfort in *all* the ways of life—our families, home, finances, commitments, and careers. God gives us a promise: "I will direct your path."

As a grandparent, I still follow these two basic principles for my life: 1) have a quiet time with my Lord each day; 2) spend at least 15 minutes each day reorganizing a part of my home. With these two guidelines I can stay on top of those things that want to get me disorganized and off track.

❧❧❧

PRAYER

Father God, I sincerely want You to direct my paths. Over the many years You have done so, and I'm blessed by the results. Encourage me to keep on keeping on. Amen.

ACTION

Activate my two basic principles of life. Give at least 30 days to your commitment.

TODAY'S WISDOM

A prayer in its simplest definition is merely a wish turned Godward.

PHILLIP BROOKS

Be a Praying Grandparent

❦❦

Dear children, let us stop just saying we love each other;
let us really show it by our actions.

1 JOHN 3:18 NLT

*T*HERE IS NO GREATER ACTION to express love for our grandchildren as to pray daily for them. In today's world they need all the hedges of protection and direction that they can get. We need also to pray for their parents daily too. Prayer is the most powerful grandparenting tool we can offer.

Finding time to pray as a parent is more challenging; as grandparents we have much more time in our schedules. We just have to make prayer our priority each day. Here are a few ways to remember when to pray:

- Walk-by prayers—If you live apart from your grandchildren, remember to pray as you walk by their pictures on the dresser or in a family photo hung on the wall. If your grandchildren are close by, you can pray as you drive to their home or as you drive by their schools.

- Write it down—In your prayer closet write down in your notebook what you want to pray for each

of the grandchildren. Don't trust your memory—
write it down. In your notebook you might want
to include a photo of each of your grandchildren;
that way you can look into their eyes and faces as
you pray.

• Support group can pray too—Ask your friends,
Bible-study members, Sunday school group to pray
for your grandchildren. The more the merrier! Let
other grandparents know you will pray for their
grandchildren if they will pray for yours.

• By your Bible reading—As you read various stories
in your daily reading, ask for the same character to
be developed in your own grandchildren: the same
courage as Daniel, Esther's faithfulness, the bold-
ness of Paul, and so forth.

• Throughout the day—The Scriptures say we are to
pray without ceasing. You can pray as you live
life—be it shopping, taking your daily walk, driv-
ing your errands, walking the dog, putting on your
makeup, brushing your teeth, or even taking a
shower.

❧❧

PRAYER

*F*ather God, You know the desires of my heart. I
truly want to be a prayer warrior for my grandchildren. I plead to You for their salvation and their daily

walk with You. May they feel and touch Your goodness in their lives. Protect them from any harm.
Amen.

ACTION

*P*ut your desire into action. Don't just talk about
praying for these little ones (or big ones), but take
time to do it!

TODAY'S WISDOM

*E*ach man has a choice in life. He may approach life
as a creator, as a critic, a lover or a hater, a giver or a
taker.

AUTHOR UNKNOWN

From
Grammy's Kitchen

Chicken Tostadas

Ingredients

Refried beans
Yogurt
Sour cream
Guacamole
Chicken, cooked and shredded
Cheddar cheese, grated
Tomatoes
Lettuce
Olives
Parsley
Corn tortillas

Preparation

1. Prepare all ingredients in desired amounts.
2. Bake corn tortillas, 1 per serving: Place directly on oven rack, single layer, in a 350° oven for 10 to 12 minutes.
3. Arrange ingredients on each crispy tortilla in the following order:

   ⅓ to ½ cup refried beans
   1 cup shredded lettuce, mixed dark leafy and iceberg
   2 tablespoons to ¼ cup grated cheddar cheese
   ¼ cup to ½ cup guacamole
   1 to 2 tablespoons yogurt and sour cream blend (half and half)
   5 cherry tomatoes or ½ tomato cut in wedges
   3 to 6 whole ripe olives
   sprigs of fresh parsley

A Household Hint for the Kitchen

Keep a small plastic shaker bottle (such as sea-soned salt comes in) filled with baking soda with dishwashing supplies. It is handy to take a stain out of a coffee cup or polish chrome-finished small appliances while washing dishes. Be sure to clearly label the bottle.

Live for Today

❧❧

*May the God of hope fill you with
all joy and peace as you trust in him,
so that you may overflow with hope
by the power of the Holy Spirit.*

Romans 15:13 NIV

*A*s I've observed my five grandchildren over the years, one thing stands out very vividly: their ability to live and enjoy the moment. They can take the "now" and make it a gift. So I'm working on trying to forget about what happened yesterday and what might happen tomorrow and just experiencing the fullness of today.

In order to capture the present, we need to give less attention to worries, mistakes, what's going wrong, general concerns, things to get done, the past, the future, and the undone. *Today I will only think about today. No regrets for the past or fears about the future.* When you do this, all your focus is on the now. You can smile, laugh, pray, think, and enjoy what each moment brings.

Often our anxieties are about situations we have no control over. I tell the ladies at my time-management seminars that 85 percent of the things we worry about never happen. Why spend all that energy on something that probably will never occur?

We are to stop and smell the roses, hear the train whistle, see the puffy clouds in the sky, hear the rain fall, and watch snow flurries. When we begin to see and experience every minute, we will also begin to see the grandeur of God.

PRAYER

*F*ather God, help me live for the now. I truly want to observe all that You have given me. Amen.

ACTION

*B*uy, taste, and enjoy an ice-cream cone.

TODAY'S WISDOM

*D*oing little things with a strong desire to please God makes them really great.

St. Francis de Sales[15]

Know Where
the Line Is Drawn

*We make our decisions, and then
our decisions turn around and make us.*

F.W. Boreham

*E*ven as grandparents, we never get too old to stop making decisions. Every day begins a new day of decision making. We are the culmination of all of our decisions up to this very moment in time. The past decisions determine who we are today, and today's decisions shape our tomorrows. For each of our lives there is a line that's drawn in the sand—a moral, ethical line. If we stand on the "right" side of the line, we get to be at peace with ourselves and we have a tranquil life. If, however, we cross the line, there will be consequences to live with. Our only saving grace is that maturity should be a big help in staying on this side of the line.

> The judge looked down from the bench and, in a somber voice, declared, "Mr. Wilson, this is your day of reckoning!" Then he sentenced him to seven and one-half years in federal prison.
>
> In response, Wilson's lawyer requested that he be allowed a few minutes with his family and friends before surrendering to the authorities.

The judge replied, "Mr. Wilson is going to be taken by the marshals right now. You should have thought of that before."

Wilson was one of four California men convicted of financial fraud and sentenced to prison in this particular case. Five men were originally investigated, but the fifth, Mark Jacobs, was not arrested and charged.

Jacobs had been invited to join the financial scheme by four friends (the men sent to jail) in a weekly Bible study. They had assured him their plan was totally legal. Yet something inside Jacobs said it wasn't right. While it was hard to say no to good friends, he chose to go with his conscience and told them he wouldn't participate.

The lawyers for the four convicted men pleaded with the judge that their clients had simply made mistakes of poor judgment. They were good men who loved their wives and kids, gave to charities, and were active in their churches. The crime involved a "gray" area, crossing a moral line that wasn't clear.

The judge disagreed. "It is not hard to determine where the line is," he said. "The guy who drew the line is Mark Jacobs. He knew what was right and what was wrong, and he didn't hesitate. Hopefully, now we will have fewer people who are willing to walk up to the line and dabble with going over the line. We will have people like Mr. Jacobs, who wouldn't touch this thing with a ten-foot pole."[16]

Too often we see men and women in responsible positions who don't know where to draw the line. We see it in the worlds of high finance, religion, politics, entertainment, and sports. Our society's ethics and morality are no longer firmly anchored in the Judeo-Christian principles of our forefathers. Without these guidelines to show where to draw the line, people get confused and become adrift when it comes to knowing right from wrong. But as Christians, we have God's Word as a solid, trustworthy source of truth and standards.

In 1 Peter 1:6-7, we are reminded that we become pure just as gold does. It's a *process*. As one writer explains, "Gold has to be heated and reheated and reheated several times for the alloys and impurities to be brought to the surface, where the goldsmith can remove them. If you forget that becoming pure is a process, you risk becoming overwhelmed by discouragement when you experience those inevitable setbacks."[17]

Wanting to be pure in a world of gray isn't enough. We have to *develop a plan of action* if we are going to become more like Jesus. We don't look down to see the line in the sand—we continually look up. Yes, even grandparents have to be on guard to make sure they make the right decisions. We need to...

- guard our hearts (Matthew 6:21)
- guard our minds (Colossians 3:2)
- guard our eyes (Job 31:1)
- guard the little things (Luke 16:10)

PRAYER

*F*ather God, I come before You concerned about how I can live a pure life. I want to make correct decisions. May I continue to look to You for guidance. Amen.

ACTION

*H*ave your spouse or a close friend hold you accountable for the decisions you make.

TODAY'S WISDOM

*Y*our capacity to say "no" determines your capacity to say "yes" to greater things.

E. STANLEY JONES

The War Against Values

❧❧❧

All things are lawful for me,
but not all things are profitable.

1 CORINTHIANS 6:12

As a grandparent, I can't believe the difference in American values now versus when I was raising my children. But when our grandchildren are with us in our environment, we are responsible for what they take in.

One of the greatest influences that impacts our thinking is the media. Unfortunately, the media in America is mostly controlled by secular humanists, so the slant of most print copy, programming, advertising, and news portrays a secular lifestyle. What is secular humanism? It's the view that man establishes his own moral values apart from the influence of anyone, including God, and the individual determines his own destiny. The individual becomes the "master of his own fate."

The problem with such a life view is that it has no absolutes. Everything is relative; there is no eternal reference point. People can make up their own rules as they go. How do we know if sexual promiscuity is immoral or not? Why shouldn't we cheat in business? Why should family life be considered more important than a career?

Ted Koppel, the news anchor for ABC's *Nightline,* in a commencement address at Duke University, said: "We have reconstructed the Tower of Babel, and it is a television antenna—a thousand voices producing a daily parody of democracy in which everyone's opinion is afforded equal weight regardless of substance or merit. This means we need to guard our minds more carefully because so many kooky ideas are floating around."

Perhaps the only way to overcome this impact is to reevaluate our sources of entertainment and information. We should be concerned that our subconscious minds might be swayed in unwanted viewing. As grandparents we have the opportunity to screen what will be heard and seen in our homes. After all, all TV sets have an "on" and "off" button. Don't be apologetic. There are some wonderful alternative activities for when the grandchildren come for a visit or a sleepover.

ॐॐ

PRAYER

*F*ather God, let me use the opportunity when my grandchildren come to make it a rewarding visit. Let just being together be a wonderful expression of love for each other. Help me correctly filter what they see and hear in my house. Amen.

ACTION

*G*o to a Christian bookstore and select some wholesome videos or DVDs for when the grandchildren come to visit.

TODAY'S WISDOM

*L*ife is an adventure of faith, if we are to be victors over it, not victims of it. Faith in the God above us, faith in the little infinite soul within us, faith in life and in our fellow souls—without faith, the plus quality, we cannot really live.

JOSEPH FORT NEWTON

SPIRIT LIFTERS

♥ Make your kitchen a place that says welcome. A bowl of freshly washed lemons as a centerpiece is a great way to say hello.

♥ Store foods in ways that allow them to be decorative as well as useful. Display fruit in a basket or in a special bowl on the kitchen table or drain board. Stack potatoes and onions in a basket, and use it to enliven an out-of-the-way corner of your counter or floor.

♥ Instead of putting the catsup bottle on a table, serve catsup in a little crock with a small spoon.

♥ Place photos of you with your guest on the bedside table in the guest room.

Never Give Up

We never give up. Though our bodies are dying,
our inner strength in the Lord is growing every day.

2 Corinthians 4:16 TLB

*I*F YOU HAVE FINANCIAL TROUBLES, setbacks...it's not the end.

If you have been lied to and deceived...it's not the end.

If you have lost your job...it's not the end.

If you have lost your home...it's not the end.

If something has been stolen from you or if you have been robbed of your inheritance...it's not the end.

If you have a child who is ensnared in sin, entangled in a web of wrong relationships, failing according to life's report card, or refusing to communicate with you...it's not the end.

If your mate has walked away, chosen someone else instead of you...it's not the end.

If you have just lost a loved one to death—sudden death,

expected or unexpected—it's not the end. Even if your loved one committed suicide…it's not the end.

If you are incarcerated for a crime—it's not the end.

If you are losing your hearing or your sight—it's not the end.

If you are in the depths of depression, if you are battling depression or a chemical imbalance that has thrown all your emotions and even your way of doing things out of kilter…it's not the end.

If you have learned that you have a terminal disease, a crippling disease, a wasting disease…it's not the end.

If you have stepped onto the threshold of death…it's not the end.

I can tell you all this with the utmost of confidence and know that what I am telling you is truth.

It may seem like the end…

You may wish it were the end…

But it is not the end because God is God and the end has not yet come.[18]

ର୍ଗ୍ର

PRAYER

*F*ather God, thank You again for assuring me that this isn't the end, for the end will be an "eternal weight of glory" far beyond all comparison. I trust

You for perfecting what's taking place in my life.
Amen.

ACTION

In your journal, list several of your temporary afflic-
tions. Beside each one, write, "This is producing an
eternal weight of glory for me."

TODAY'S WISDOM

*G*randparenting is a marvelous opportunity to keep
alive, alert, growing, and giving.

FITZHUH DODSON

Specially and
Wonderfully Made

❧❧

I will give thanks to You,
for I am fearfully and wonderfully made.
PSALM 139:14

*I*N A RECENT STUDY, THE FINDINGS WERE that a large percentage
of young and old do not realize that they are unique and
special. We look in the mirror and see back the negatives—
wrinkles aren't where they were last month, my jaws are beginning to sag. My eyes are drooping, I've got more gray hair than
ever before. Time has a way of telling us we are getting older.
But even with the physical evidence of change, we can charge
into the grandparenting phase of our life with the knowledge
that in God's eyes we are special and wonderfully made.

You're special. In all the world there's nobody like
you.

Since the beginning of time there has never been
another person like you.

Nobody has your smile, nobody has your eyes,
your nose, your hair, your hands, your voice.

You're special.

No one can be found who has your handwriting.

Nobody anywhere has your tastes for food, clothing, music or art.

No one sees things just as you do.

In all of time there's been no one who laughs like you, no one who cries like you, and what makes you cry or laugh will never produce identical laughter and tears from anybody else, ever.

You're the only one in all of creation who has your set of abilities.

Oh, there will always be somebody who is better at one of the things you're good at, but no one in the universe can reach the quality of your combination of talents, ideas, abilities and feelings. Like a room full of musical instruments, some may excel alone, but none can match the symphony sound when all are played together. You're a symphony.

Through all of eternity, no one will ever look, talk, walk, think or do like you.

You're special...you're rare. And in all rarity there is great value. Because of your great value you need not attempt to imitate others...you will accept—yes, celebrate your differences.

You're special and you're beginning to realize it's no accident that you're special.

You're beginning to see that God made you special for a purpose.

He must have a job for you that no one else can do as well as you.

Out of the billions of applicants, only one is qualified, only one has the right combination of what it takes.

That one is you, because…you're special.[19]

Someone in your life may need to hear these words today. Maybe that someone is you. Do you, like the psalmist, fully realize that you are "fearfully and wonderfully made"? Be sure to express this truth not only to yourself, but to all your loved ones—especially your spouse, your children, and your grandchildren.

We have a tradition in our home that reinforces this concept—it's called "The You Are Special Red Plate." We use this plate for breakfasts, lunches, dinners, birthdays, anniversaries, and various other events. We've used it at home, in restaurants, at the park, and on the beach. We have every person at the event tell the person being honored why that person is special to them. Then we give the special person a chance to share why he or she thinks he (she) is special. The comments are amazing. On many occasions we have had grown men shed a tear because no one has ever told them why they are special.

Our red plate tradition is very valuable in our family—and it will be the same in your family! We all need to be reminded now and then that we are special.

⁂

PRAYER

Father God, help me realize that I am Your handiwork; therefore, I am very special in Your sight. You knew me before I was made. Thank You for Your amazing love. Amen.

ACTION

List in your journal three things that make you special.

TODAY'S WISDOM

There are two ways to live life. One is as though nothing is a miracle. The other is as though everything is a miracle.

ALBERT EINSTEIN

Winning the Race

❧❧❧

Let endurance have its perfect result,
so that you may be perfect
and complete, lacking in nothing.

JAMES 1:4

A HARE WAS ONE DAY MAKING FUN OF a tortoise for being so slow on his feet.

"Wait a bit," said the tortoise. "I'll run a race with you, and I'll wager that I win."

"Oh, well," replied the hare, who was much amused at the idea. "Let's try and see."

It was soon agreed that the fox should set a course for them and be the judge. When the time came, both started off together, but the hare was soon so far ahead he thought he might as well have a rest; so down he lay and fell fast asleep. Meanwhile the tortoise kept plodding on and reached the goal. At last the hare woke up with a start and dashed to the finish line, only to find that the tortoise had already won the race.

—An Aesop fable

Too many of us only see the start of the race. So much of life is painted with speed, flash, and sizzle that we can be intimidated.

A few years ago our family went to Lake Tahoe to ski during the Christmas break. As we walked on the icy slopes of this beautiful resort, our eyes were full of the best—the best cars, skis, clothes, and beauty. We couldn't believe our eyes! We had never seen so much sizzle in one place. So I said to myself, "No way am I going to compete with them." After being coaxed into my group ski lesson, I found that members of the sizzle group were also in my class, and they couldn't ski any better than I could!

Today's Scripture teaches that perseverance is enduring with patience. In the Bible, perseverance describes Christians who remain steadfast in the face of opposition, attack, and discouragement. When we persevere with patience, we exhibit our ability to stay faithful with calmness and without complaint. As believers we must daily commit ourselves to godly living.

Commitment and discipline are not words "the world" is comfortable with. The new millennium wants everything to feel good—but perseverance doesn't always feel good. It sometimes demands denial of self and pain. That's why trusting and having faith in God's guidance is so important.

Scripture is clear. It teaches we are to persevere—

- in prayer (Ephesians 6:18)
- in obedience (Revelation 14:12)
- in self-control (2 Peter 1:5-7)

Scripture promises us certain blessings if we endure:

- final deliverance (Matthew 24:13)
- rewarded faith (Hebrews 11:6)
- eternal inheritance (Revelation 21:7)

As we live out our lives and persevere daily against all the trials and temptations, we are rewarded by the Lord with the fruit of His Spirit for all eternity (see Galatians 5:22-23):

- love
- joy
- peace
- goodness
- faithfulness

- gentleness
- patience
- kindness
- self-contorl

PRAYER

*F*ather God, in life's difficulties help me look to You to see what You are trying to teach me. Amen.

ACTION

*J*ot down several struggles you are having in life. Beside each one, list several things that God is trying to teach you through them.

TODAY'S WISDOM

*O*n the first report of illness or accident, send a get-well card. Mail the card the same day, and follow up with a short telephone call to check how the grand-child is feeling.

From Grammy's Kitchen

Sloppy Joes

Serves 12

Sauce

    1 chopped onion
    2 tablespoons butter
    2 cups hot water
    1 pound hamburger
    ½ cup catsup
    ⅓ cup barbecue sauce
    1 tablespoon Worcestershire sauce
    1 tablespoon mustard
    ¼ cup sweet pickle relish
    2 slices lemon
    12 burger buns, split in halves

Directions

1. Sauté onion in butter.

2. Add remaining ingredients.

3. Slow cook for 1–2 hours.

4. Remove lemon slices before serving.

5. To serve, spoon sauce over split buns. Replace tops.

A Household Hint for the Kitchen

To speed up a sluggish drain, first run hot tap water down the drain, then pour in 3 tablespoons of baking soda and ½ cup distilled white vinegar. Stop up the drain and wait 15 minutes. The baking soda and vinegar will foam up, reacting with each other and will eat away at whatever is slowing the drain. Finally, flush the drain with hot tap water.

Contentment

❧❧

But godliness actually is
a means of great gain
when accompanied by contentment.

1 TIMOTHY 6:6

RECENTLY I WAS VISITING OUR GRANDCHILD, Bradley Joe Barnes II. As I was holding him, rubbing my hands through his hair, tracing the shape of his toes and fingers, my mind went to thinking about what he was going to be as he grew to manhood. Was he going to have good grades and go to college? Would he be a fireman, a pastor, a teacher, a coach, a salesman? Suddenly I realized that I was thinking about *what* he could be rather than focusing my thoughts and prayers on *who* he would be.

In today's culture we are all drawn away from spiritual pursuits to putting our hope into wealth (1 Timothy 6:17) and to building our lives around ways to accomplish this ambition. As I sat there in Bradley Joe's room, I began praying that his extended family might teach him higher values than money, career, and fame. Not that these are evil, but the value we place on them can lead to our downfall (1 Timothy 6:9).

In today's passage Paul states, "Godliness with contentment is great gain." When we find ourselves looking to the future because we aren't content with today, may God give us a peace of mind that lets us rest where He has placed us. Be content in today![20]

As grandparents, our children and grandchildren learn contentment by what they see in our lives. If we live in peace, so will they. If we live with love, so will they; if we live with joy, so will they; if we have patience, so will they; if we are kind, so will they be. If there is goodness in our hearts, it will be in theirs; if faithfulness is obvious, they will have it; if we are gentle, so will they be; if we exhibit self-control, so will they. Yes, those around us will live by what they see.

If you want your family to be content—then live it!

❦❦❦

PRAYER

*F*ather God, give me contentment so that my loved ones see that I am happy in all I have. I want my loved ones to live a life of contentment. Amen.

ACTION

*W*rite a letter to God thanking Him for all your blessings. Name them one by one.

TODAY'S WISDOM

Contentment comes out of the capacity to feel deeply, to enjoy simply, to think freely, to risk life, to be needed, and to be thankful for all that God has given you.

AUTHOR UNKNOWN

What Is a Home?

There is no spectacle on earth more appealing
than that of a beautiful woman
in the act of cooking dinner for someone she loves.

THOMAS WOLFE

WHAT'S THE DIFFERENCE BETWEEN a house and a home? We hear people interchange these two words all the time. But those of us who are fortunate to live in a home know the difference. "Home" is not simply four walls with a roof overhead. It's not just a structure in an upscale neighborhood (in fact many homes are found in the poorer neighborhoods of a city). It doesn't have to have a certain architectural style or construction (many are just plain homes—nothing fancy).

Home is a state of mind, built with more than bricks and mortar. Home is always built with a lot of love. The collective size of the hearts of the people inside is more important than the size of the building.

A home is a place where we know we are protected and loved. It is a "trauma center" where hurt people can get well. It is a place where freedom rings. The occupants don't have to be shaped with the same cookie cutter. Each person is encouraged to grow in his or her own direction for life. In this place called home, we can cry when we are sad and laugh with shouts of joy when we have victories.

This wonderful haven called home is where we gather to celebrate life. Traditions are carried on, parties are held for special events, and food flows as much as love. When the children leave home they are always glad to come back home. There is no other place on earth that feels as good as being home.

PRAYER

*F*ather God, thank You so much for giving me the desire to create a home for my family. Help me make my house into a home—a place where my children and grandchildren always love to come to. I am truly receiving all of Your blessings for being a homemaker. Amen.

ACTION

*I*f you only have a house, begin making it a home. Look around and check your house and your heart. Does anything need changed or adjusted? Make the alterations, and then be patient. It takes time to create a home.

TODAY'S WISDOM

*H*ouses are built of brick and stones, but homes are made of love alone.

AUTHOR UNKNOWN

□ □ □

Pray Earnestly
for Your Grandchildren

*Pray till prayer makes you forget your own wish,
and leave it or merge it into God's will.*

FREDRICK W. ROBERTSON

*N*O MATTER IF YOU LIVE NEAR or far away, you can be faithful in daily prayer for your precious grandchildren and for their parents. As children are raised and look back on what kept them on the straight and narrow, they recall the assurance of a praying parent and/or grandparent.

Prayer is so powerful—many times far more than our own understanding. We know by experience that God listens and acts upon believers' prayers. Often we don't see immediate changes, but God's clock runs on a different time than we do.

Scripture gives us many verses to engrain in our daily prayer lives. One thing about children and grandchildren, they both give us plenty of opportunities to pray! A wise person told me once, "When children are young you talk to them about Jesus, and when they get older you talk to Jesus about them." Such an enlightening remark. Don't give up praying for your whole family, though.

As you talk to the Lord, pray that your grandchildren:

• fear the Lord and serve Him (Deuteronomy 6:13)

- know Christ as Savior early in life (Psalm 63:1)
- desire the right kind of friends (Proverbs 1:10,15)
- will be saved for the right mate (2 Corinthians 6:14)
- submit totally to God (James 4:7-8)
- stay protected from wrong people or wrong places (Hosea 2:6-7)
- honor their parents (Exodus 20:12)

☙❧

PRAYER

*F*ather God, give me conviction to earnestly pray for my children and grandchildren every day. With all that's happening in the world today, they need a hedge around all the areas of life. Hold me accountable. Amen.

ACTION

*T*ake one of the seven areas of prayer each week and concentrate upon that particular phase of your grandchildren's lives. On the eighth week start over again.

TODAY'S WISDOM

May the wisdom of God instruct me,
the eye of God watch over me,
the ear of God hear me,
the word of God give me sweet talk,
the hand of God defend me,
the way of God guide me.
Christ be with me.
Christ before me.
Christ in me.
Christ under me.
Christ over me.
Christ on my right hand.
Christ on my left hand.
Christ on this side.
Christ on that side.
Christ in the head of everyone to whom I speak.
Christ in the mouth of every person who speaks to me.
Christ in the eye of every person who looks upon me.
Christ in the ear of everyone who hears me today. Amen.

ST. PATRICK

☐ ☐ ☐

The Perfect Manual

But where can wisdom be found?
And where is the place of understanding?
JOB 28:12

NOT LONG AGO MY FRIEND Florence Littauer wrote a book titled _Looking for Love in All the Wrong Places._ And it's true. We do that. We seek wisdom in places where there is no wisdom by talking to friends, reading magazines, listening to talk shows, and attending seminars. We live in a culture that has a difficult time reading the instruction manual—the Bible. For some reason we want to invent the wheel by ourselves. We have trouble seeking the truth from the wise.

The writer of the book of Job struggled with knowing what to do. In Job 28:12 he asked, "Where can wisdom be found?" All through chapter 28 he searches for the answer:

- man doesn't know its value (verse 13)
- it is not found in the land of the living (13)
- the inner earth says, "It's not in me" (14)
- the sea says, "It's not in me (14)
- you can't buy it with gold or silver (15)
- precious stones don't have it (16)

- it can't be equated with gold (17)
- pearls don't have it (18)
- it is hidden from the eyes of all living creatures (21)
- God understands its way, and He knows its place (23)
- God looks to the ends of the earth and sees everything under heaven (24)
- God saw wisdom and declared it (27)
- God established it and searched it out (27)

Job and his friends claimed wisdom of themselves, but wisdom is clearly an outgrowth of God and not merely something to be obtained. Although we can know and understand many things, we cannot attain the level of Creator wisdom. There will always be questions that only God can answer. Solomon knew that true wisdom is not found in human understanding but is from God alone. The fear of the Lord is wisdom (see Proverbs 1:7; 9:10).[21]

ഔൟഔ

PRAYER

*F*ather God, let my eyes skip over the wisdom written in secular magazines. Let my eyes and heart go directly to Your Word to find the wisdom I need. Your light will guide me. Amen.

ACTION

*R*ead Job 28. Jot down in your journal some thoughts on where wisdom can be found.

TODAY'S WISDOM

*T*he road to wisdom? Well, it's plain and simple to express: Err and err and err again but less and less and less.

PIET HEIN

SPIRIT LIFTERS

♥ Hang a bright banner by your door to say hello to everyone who comes to visit your home.

♥ Collect perfume samples and scented inserts from magazine ads to freshen your drawers or suitcases. Or try spraying your perfume on the drawer liners to give a scent of you.

♥ Try using plants as architectural helps—a group of tall plants to divide a room, for instance, or a combination of potted and hanging plants to partially screen a window.

Good vs. Evil

୨୧୨୧

Blessed are the poor in spirit,
for theirs is the kingdom of heaven.
MATTHEW 5:3

*A*s GRANDPARENTS WE MUST ALWAYS be on the alert to be teachers of truth. Youngsters love to hear stories about good guys versus bad guys. History is full of stories telling how good overcomes evil.

When I was a girl, my brother and I loved to listen to the radio series *The Lone Ranger.* Believe it or not, I learned a lot of good life principles from that program. To this day, when I hear the "William Tell Overture," my mind immediately flashes back to this great program that gave me my first exposure to good and evil.

What was this masked man's secret for success? The Lone Ranger believed in...

- tolerance—The acceptance of other races through his close friendship with the Native American Tonto.

- fairness—Advocating the American tradition, which gives each person the right to choose a lifework and earn profit in proportion to individual effort.

- patriotism—Love of country, which meant more than flag-waving and answering the call of war. It included aiding churches, serving the community, preserving law and order, and maintaining a proper home for bringing up the next generation of good citizens.

- sympathy—Choosing the side of the oppressed in time of need. Demonstrating a strong man can be tender, the Lone Ranger is ever-forgiving.

- religion—The right to worship God in individual ways. While the Lone Ranger was visualized as a protestant, his confidantes were the Native American Tonto and the Catholic padre.

As grandparents we have the opportunity to teach life-lasting virtues to our grandchildren. Always be on the alert for times to talk about the importance of knowing the differences between good and evil. Even though we don't use silver bullets, we can learn to use silver words.[22]

PRAYER

*F*ather God, when I'm with my grandchildren, help me teach them virtues based on Your Word. Let one of my legacies be that I was a teacher of life. Amen.

ACTION

Call or e-mail your grandchildren today. Share with them one virtue you would like them to adopt as their own.

TODAY'S WISDOM

Make preparations in advance. You never have trouble if you are prepared for it.

THEODORE ROOSEVELT

Walk Together in Wisdom

❦

*For he will not often consider the years
of his life, because God keeps him occupied
with the gladness of his heart.*

ECCLESIASTES 5:20

SOMETIMES WE WALK INTO the golden years and find out they aren't so golden. Where the mirror and photographers were once our friends, we now realize they have become our enemies. The person we see in the mirror looks more like our parent. Where we used to find ourselves in photos, we now don't even want pictures taken—no more mirrors and no more photographs.

One of the great values of these golden years is that we get senior citizen discounts in all areas of life, we can belong to AARP, and we qualify for Social Security and Medicare. Along with the good, we put up with comments such as:

- Let me help you with your bag.
- Shall I get valet parking for you?
- Are you still working?
- The grocer checker wants to know if he can help you with your groceries.
- Should we take the elevator to the second floor?

- Be careful when you step off the curb.
- Be sure to look both ways before you cross the street.

These make us feel like we're still in kindergarten. All of a sudden we've become useless and invisible.

Who and what is that person God wants me to be—at this stage of my life? As a grandparent, I want to pursue what God has for me right this moment. Except for the mirror and photograph, I haven't felt better in years. I'm eager to take on the world (at least I have opinions on everything). I am more able to take on the giants of life because God keeps me occupied with gladness in my heart.

You have the opportunity to be an encouragement to those around you. People want to have you share some of the secrets of contentment. Being a grandparent gives you the opportunity to really shape the next generation. Your love, your connection, your encouragements, your support cannot be delivered by anyone but you. The gladness in your heart is what makes today so much fun. You can hardly wait to get out of bed to see what God has in store for you.

PRAYER

*F*ather God, Your Word encourages my heart to be filled with joy. My days are not lonely because I am continuing to be the person You want me to be. Amen.

ACTION

*D*o something today that will make your heart happy.

TODAY'S WISDOM

*T*he role of teacher is one of the most important for any grandparent.

ARTHUR KARNHABER

Teaching by Example

❦❦❦

I exhort you, be imitators of me.
1 CORINTHIANS 4:16

ONE NIGHT WHEN A GRANDFATHER was praying with his grandson, the boy asked a very penetrating question.

"Granddad, have I ever met a Christian?"

The grandfather was taken aback, realizing that his grandson had not caught what he was attempting to teach the lad.

Are you living for Christ in a way that you are modeling Christ to your children and grandchildren?

In bygone days a father who was a skilled tradesman would take on his son as an apprentice. This required many years of training so the apprentice could qualify as a journeyman. This was teaching by example. There are very few trades that are taught like that anymore; vocations have become far too complex.

However, in the family setting, children still learn by example. They learn by seeing mom, dad, and grandparents in action. They see the adults' values and ethics put into practice.

Your "little apprentices" are watching everything you do in the car, at a ball game, in church, around the meal table—everywhere! These are great opportunities to teach your grandchildren the important values of life. Children's eyes are always open to example.[23]

※※※

PRAYER

*F*ather God, thanks for the reminder that my grandchildren are looking to me to help them become good adults. Amen.

ACTION

*S*pend quality time with your grandchildren today. Let them see and hear you make godly decisions.

TODAY'S WISDOM

A group of two hundred executives were asked what makes a person successful. Eighty percent listed enthusiasm as the most important quality.

SOURCE UNKNOWN

Always Means Always

~~

*[Love] always protects, always trusts,
always hopes, always perseveres.*

1 Corinthians 13:7 NIV

*I*t's very hard for us mere mortals to grasp "always." In today's culture, we don't adequately understand this kind of commitment. When we say "always," don't we usually mean sometimes...or most of the time? But "always" really means eternal and everlasting. Can anyone commit to "always"?

When Scripture says "always," it means always—never changing, dependable until death. We as grandparents are challenged when Paul writes that love:

- always protects
- always trusts
- always hopes
- always perseveres

As grandparents, we so want our family to honor us with this kind of love, and we also want to be known to honor and respect them with the same intensity of love. When grandpa or grandma says something, they can take it to the bank. We

126

want to be known as people who do what we say we are going to do. Not sometimes but *always*.

As we become older and look back over life's journey, may we know that love and what it encompasses is indeed the true victory of life.

❧

PRAYER

*F*ather God, give us the strength and perseverance to truthfully say without hesitation that we will *always* love our family with the "always" principle.

ACTION

*L*et your family be assured that you will always love them.

TODAY'S WISDOM

*H*e who would have beautiful roses in his garden must have beautiful roses in his heart. He must love them well and always. He must have not only the glowing admiration, the enthusiasm, and the passion, but the tenderness, the thoughtfulness, the reverence, the watchfulness of love.

S.R. Hole

From
Grammy's Kitchen

How to Hard Boil an Egg

Hard-boiled eggs are great travelers—just be sure to pack a little salt and pepper. You can make just one egg by this recipe, but you might as well make more and have some extras for tuna salad. This is also the way to prepare Easter eggs for dyeing.

Ingredients

> 1 large egg
> Water

How to Make It

1. Put the egg in the bottom of a saucepan that has a tight lid. Add cold water deep enough to cover the egg completely, plus a little more.

2. Place on the stove and turn on heat to medium high. Let heat for about 5 or 10 minutes, then turn up heat to high.

3. When water boils, put the lid on the saucepan and remove the whole thing from the stove. Put the pan on a heatproof surface and let it stand covered for 10 minutes. Then take the pan to the sink and drain off the hot water. Run cold water in the pan for several minutes to stop the egg from cooking. Store it in the refrigerator until ready to eat.

A Household Hint for the Kitchen

Have fresh lemon juice all year long. Squeeze excess lemons and freeze juice in ice cube trays. Transfer the frozen cubes into Baggies and defrost for fresh lemon juice any time!

A Balanced Home

Unless the LORD builds the house,
they labor in vain who build it;
unless the LORD guards the city,
the watchman keeps awake in vain.

PSALM 127:1

*A*S GRANDPARENTS WE SOMETIMES WONDER if we actually have a home—or is it merely a stopover place to eat, do laundry, hang around, and sleep? Is it just a place to repair things, mow the lawn, paint, wallpaper, and install new carpet? A true home is much more than all that. It is a place of people living, growing, laughing, crying, learning, and creating together.

A small child, after watching his house burn down, was quoted as saying, "We still have a home. We just don't have a house to put it in." How perceptive!

Our home should be a trauma center for the whole family. It's a place where healing occurs and peace reigns. We don't have to be perfect—just forgiven. We can grow, we can make mistakes, we can shout for joy, we can cry, we can agree, and we can disagree. Home is a place where happy experiences occur. It's a place sheltered from the problems of the world, a place of love, acceptance, and security.

When we read newspapers, we are confronted with tragedies around us, and we realize that the world outside our front door is falling apart. But within our four walls we can offer a place of peace.

What can we do to have a home like God intended? As with everything in life, when something is broken we go back to the instruction book—and life's manual is the Bible. The home is God's idea. He designed the home to be the foundation of society—a place to meet the mental, spiritual, physical, and emotional needs of people.

The members of a family must work together to make their house a true home—not just a place where they live. Solomon spoke to this subject in Proverbs 24:3-4. He outlines three basic principles of building a balanced home:

- wisdom
- understanding
- knowledge

It is impossible to create a home by our own efforts; we aren't strong enough to accomplish the task. We must guide our hearts, souls, and lives to God's Son, Jesus Christ. He is our source of strength.[24]

PRAYER

Father God, give my family and me wisdom, understanding, and knowledge. Help me turn my house into a home. Amen.

ACTION

*P*ray for your home and your family members.

TODAY'S WISDOM

*T*he team that makes the most mistakes will probably win. The doer makes mistakes, and I want doers on my team, players who make things happen.

JOHN WOODEN

The Gift

∽∾∽

For all things come from You,
and from Your hand we have given You.

1 CHRONICLES 29:14

BEING A "GIVER" IS MUCH MORE rewarding than being a "taker" of a gift. There is seldom a time when we receive a gift, other than on special occasions. When we have the opportunity to be with our grandchildren, we are able to give and give and give love. What a joy to give them love!

Long ago, imagine what a heavy schedule of appointments President Abraham Lincoln had to keep day after day. Yet when an elderly grandmother with no official business in mind asked to see him, he graciously consented. As she entered his office, he rose to greet her and asked how he might be of service. She replied that she had not come to ask a favor. She had heard that the president liked a certain kind of cookie, so she had baked some for him and brought them to his office.

With tears in his eyes, Lincoln responded, "You are the very first person who has ever come into my office asking not, expecting not, but rather bringing me a gift. I thank you from the bottom of my heart."

I know I get so excited when my children and grandchildren

give me a gift and not a request. How much more must God rejoice when we don't bring a list of requests but instead we simply bring Him the gift of our gratitude and love. Nothing pleases our heavenly Father more than our sincere thanksgiving!

PRAYER

*F*ather God, let me continue to be a vessel that gives. I am so thankful for all the gifts You so freely give me and my family. May my family receive all the love that I offer them. Amen.

ACTION

*G*ive a gift of love to your family today.

TODAY'S WISDOM

*I*n ordinary life we hardly realize that we receive a great deal more than we give, and that it is only with great gratitude that life becomes rich. It is very easy to overestimate the importance of our own achievements in comparison with what we owe others.

DIETRICH BONHOEFFER

Enjoying Winter
with Sunshine

❧❧❧

There is an appointed time for everything.
And there is a time for every event under heaven.
ECCLESIASTES 3:1

*A*S WE ENTER THE WINTER SEASON of our lives, we look back
at the last few decades and wonder, "What if?" Much of what
happens in the previous three seasons—spring, summer, and
fall—determines what life will be like in the final season of the
year—winter. Throughout the *Farmer's Almanac,* we read
detailed descriptions about planting, reaping, and harvest-
ing—when to plant and when to rest. The fruits of sowing our
seeds are based not only on what we do but on the elements
of nature. We must be prepared to do all we can and then be
willing to let God do the rest.

Spring

In the springtime of life we plant our seeds. We are so
excited about the newness of life: courtship, a wedding, a new
job, children, a new home, and all the rest of the excitement
that comes along with spring. We are full of hope and anticipation of what life has to offer. Many times we are naïve
about what we are doing. Unless we really have it together as

a couple, we give little thought or reason to why we do what we do.

A tried-and-true farmer isn't quite as nonchalant about this season of life. He realizes that in order to have a good harvest, he must have a good spring. He must know what crop he is planting, make proper seed selection, plant after the last frost, and pray that rain or irrigation comes at the proper time.

Spring is crucial in life because what happens in these months greatly affects what the remaining three seasons of the year will be like.

One of our mottos is: "Success is progressive realization of worthwhile goals." Spring is the time of life when we begin to establish these goals.

Summer

Many times the drudgery of summer makes us lose sight of what life is all about. During these long, hot days we press on and remember why we are on this earth. It isn't by accident that we are here. Occasionally we have a thunderstorm to break the monotony of this period of life.

Spring is the freshness of newness, but summer tests us to see if we really have the discipline and godly character to see life through these difficult periods. Many would-be farmers and would-be marriages never get through this phase of life. Only those with dedicated and serious purpose survive. Life often gets boring during this season. But to get to the harvest season, we have to get through the summer.

Fall

Now fall is here—all what we have worked for so long and so hard. At last we will be able to reap the harvest of our efforts—if we have done a good job in spring and summer. "Whoever sows sparingly will also reap sparingly, and whoever sows generously will also reap generously" (2 Corinthians 9:6 NIV).

This is the season of life where we receive our blessings. In order to have abundance, we must have sowed with abundance. This is our pay period of life. In Proverbs 24:3-4, we are promised that our rooms will be filled with rare and beautiful riches. These rare and beautiful riches are our children, our grandchildren, friends, good health, emotional and psychological stability, and above all our love for the Lord—just the things we hoped for when we were in the springtime of life.

One of the warnings of this season is not to use up all of our harvest. We must save some seeds and fruits so that we will have something to plant next spring. There will be more springs, and we certainly want to be prepared when they come.

As grandparents we certainly see the importance of saving for the next spring—not only for ours, but for those of our inheritance. After all, we are raising more than one generation.

Winter

At last winter has arrived, and we have a more relaxed and easy pace around the farm. Much of the day is cool, the land is frozen, and icy wind is blowing from the plains of the north. We can spend rich times in conversing with our spouses, looking back over life with some smiles and some frowns, but generally pleased about the accomplishments of spring, summer, and fall. A good book, a CD of soft music, a nap in the afternoon, an early dinner, and off to a good night's sleep.

Isn't it cozy with just the two of us around the fireplace? We can look each other in the eyes and say, "God bless and good night—you are truly my best friend!"

Enjoy winter—it's so rejuvenating![25]

ॐ

PRAYER

*F*ather God, thank You for the seasons of life. May we realize that we must be good stewards of our seasons. Thank You for planting in us a desire to follow You and Your principles for a rich, rewarding, and meaningful life. Amen.

ACTION

*W*ith your spouse sit down and plan your goals for this winter season of your life. Write them down.

TODAY'S WISDOM

*H*e who has learned to pray has learned the greatest secret of a holy and happy life.

WILLIAM LAW

SPIRIT LIFTERS

♥ You don't have to be a little girl to love a tea party!
I love to serve my afternoon guests fragrant cinnamon
tea poured into their choices from my cup-and-saucer
collection, and my wonderful healthy oatmeal cookies.

♥ Surprise your spouse and treat him at the local soda
fountain. Don't worry about the low-carb craze. Enjoy!

♥ Serve a shift or two at your local soup kitchen or bank.
Consider volunteering on a regular basis.

Raising Healthy Grandchildren

❧❧❧

By wisdom a house is built,
and through understanding it is established;
through knowledge its rooms are
filled with rare and beautiful treasures.

PROVERBS 24:3-4 NIV

*W*ISDOM, UNDERSTANDING, AND KNOWLEDGE are essential when dealing with your grandchildren. When we live these three words, our rooms are filled with rare and beautiful treasures—children and grandchildren who are obedient, polite, considerate, good citizens, and who honor God. What parent or grandparent would not love to have these treasures?

When we are out in public and observe a healthy, functioning family, we know that they directly or indirectly have been observing these three important guidelines. How do we know? Because we can see the rewards and/or blessings of that training. The parents have rare and beautiful treasures. Is it easy to be blessed? No! It takes a lot of work and stick-to-it discipline. You have to believe in the end results. My Bob and I always go up to the parents of well-mannered children and compliment them on their efforts. When you see something good, shout it from the housetop!

Use the times you are with your treasured grandchildren as opportunities to teach. You don't have to be preachy or stern. It can be fun! Many times these children will listen to you before they will listen to their own parents. You have a great deal of influence, so don't be afraid to use your adult status with these little ones.

❧❧❧

PRAYER

*F*ather God, I truly want my home to be filled with rare and beautiful treasures. Give me wisdom, understanding, and knowledge when dealing with my grandchildren. Amen.

ACTION

*D*eclare together that you and your husband are going to help raise these young children with wisdom, understanding, and knowledge.

TODAY'S WISDOM

*C*hildren are the most wholesome part of the race, the sweetest, for they are freshest from the hand of God. Whimsical, ingenious, mischievous, they fill the world with joy and good humor. We adults live a life of apprehension as to what they will think of us; a life of defense against their terrifying energy; a life of hard work to live up to their great expectations. We put them to bed with a sense of relief—and greet them in the morning with delight and anticipation. We envy them the freshness of adventure and the discovery of life. In all these ways, children add to the wonder of being alive. In all these ways, they help to keep us young.

HERBERT HOOVER

The "How" Word

✆✆

*How blessed is the man who finds wisdom
and the man who gains understanding.*

PROVERBS 3:13

*T*HE THREE-LETTER WORD "HOW" IS a marvelous word that is used throughout Scripture. As a grandparent, we can certainly use this word time and again. However, when it is used I often add another word to express my reflection upon being a grandparent. Words such as: how blessed, how majestic, how lovely, how good, how happy, how sweet, how precious, how delightful. Truly we can use these add-on words to describe our love for these young lives that God has given us.

Bob and I often say to each other, "If we would have known that grandchildren would be so much fun, we would have had them first!" Tongue-in-cheek humor, but true. We are able to give to our grandchildren what we weren't always able to give to our own children—*time*.

Throughout Scripture we find the writers using this little word "how" to describe aspects of God's influence on mankind. For example:

- "How blessed is the man who does not walk in the counsel of the wicked" (Psalm 1:1).

- "How delightful is a timely word" (Proverbs 15:23).

- "How happy is the man whom God reproves" (Job 5:17).

- "How blessed is the man who finds wisdom" (Proverbs 3:13).

- "How precious is Your lovingkindness, O God" (Psalm 36:7).

- "How devoutly and uprightly and blamelessly we have behaved toward you" (1 Thessalonians 2:10).

- "How great a love the Father has bestowed on us, that we would be called children of God" (1 John 3:1).

- "How majestic is Your name in all the world" (Psalm 8:1).

- "How lovely are Your dwelling places" (Psalm 84:1).

- "How awesome are Your works!" (Psalm 66:3).

- "How good and how pleasant it is for brothers to dwell together in unity" (Psalm 133:1).

- "How sweet are Your words...sweeter than honey" (Psalm 119:103).

- "How unsearchable are His judgments" (Romans 11:33).

You can see that this small three-letter word is so powerful in Scripture. May you realize that it has real meaning for you as a grandparent. It hopefully helps to express your love to your grandchildren. Make it a part of your teaching time when they are in your presence.

PRAYER

*F*ather God, thank You for giving me these wonderful grandchildren. May I be wise enough to plan some valuable learning experiences for their lives. May they come to me with a teachable spirit. Amen.

ACTION

*T*ake one of these "hows" and make it come alive. Put it into motion. Be creative in how you will implement it in real life.

TODAY'S WISDOM

*N*o one imagines that a symphony is supposed to improve in quality as it goes along, or that the whole object of playing it is to reach the finale. The point of music is discovered in every moment of playing and listening to it. It is the same, I feel, with the greater part of our lives, and if we are unduly absorbed in improving them we may forget altogether to live them.

ALAN WATTS

Living Stones

❧❧

You also, as living stones, are being
built up as a spiritual house for a holy priesthood,
to offer up spiritual sacrifices acceptable
to God through Jesus Christ.

1 PETER 2:5

$\mathcal{A}$ MAN TOURING A RURAL AREA of the Far East saw a boy pulling a crude plow while an old man held the handles and guided it through the rice paddy. The visitor commented, "I suppose they are very poor."

"Yes," said his guide. "When their church was built, they wanted to give something to help but they had no money. So they sold their only ox."

In America we may not have to give up an ox and pull the plow ourselves, but there are many ways we can give. I am always amazed when I go out to a job site and see pallet after pallet of bricks and stones. They're just sitting there, not much beauty to them at all. But when I go back in a few weeks, I'm startled by what the skilled masons have done with those stones. They have become fireplaces, ornamental decorations for homes, retaining walls, and walkways.

God wants to make a "spiritual house" from all of our "living stones." Some spiritual sacrifices for the transformation will be costly, but what is gained by our giving—God's praise—is always greater than what we give.[26]

PRAYER

*F*ather God, I want my spirit to be willing to make whatever sacrifices are necessary to raise my children and grandchildren in a godly home. Give me the strength and courage to live a life where they see You through watching my life. Amen.

ACTION

*I*ntentionally give something of your life away today—either money, clothes, deeds, a sacrifice, food, whatever.

TODAY'S WISDOM

*I*t is only through the mystery of self-sacrifice that a man may find himself anew.

CARL G. JUNG

God Isn't Finished
with You Yet

ৰ৹২৯

Consider it all joy, my brethren, when you
encounter various trials, knowing that
the testing of your faith produces endurance.

JAMES 1:2-3

THE LONGER WE LIVE, THE GREATER CHANCES are that we are going to have trials in our lives. As grandparents, we have lived long enough to experience many of these problems in life. We know very well that life is not always perfect. One of the great roles that we play in our family's development is to reflect peace, stability, and calmness. How do we handle these testings? The world usually gets uptight and asks a lot of "why" questions. But those who are mature in the Lord can see the big picture and realize that we are in God's will for our lives. We have a broader understanding of God's master plan for each of us.

> There was a couple who used to go to England to shop in the beautiful stores. This was their twenty-fifth wedding anniversary. They both liked antiques and pottery...and especially teacups. One day in this beautiful shop they saw a beautiful teacup. They said, "May we see that? We've never seen one quite so beautiful." As the lady handed it to them, suddenly the teacup spoke.

"You don't understand," it said. "I haven't always been a teacup. There was a time when I was red, and I was clay. My master took me and rolled me and patted me over and over and I yelled out, 'Let me alone,' but he only smiled, 'Not yet.'

"Then I was placed on a spinning wheel," the teacup said, "and suddenly I was spun around and around and around. 'Stop it! I'm getting dizzy!' I screamed. But the master only nodded and said, 'Not yet.'

"Then he put me in the oven. I never felt such heat. I wondered why he wanted to burn me, and I yelled, and I knocked at the door. I could see him through the opening and I could read his lips as he shook his head, 'Not yet.'

"Finally the door opened, he put me on the shelf, and I began to cool. 'There, that's better,' I said. And he brushed and painted me all over. The fumes were horrible. I thought I would gag. 'Stop it, stop it!' I cried. He only nodded, 'Not yet.'

"Then suddenly he put me back into the oven, not like the first one. This was twice as hot, and I knew I would suffocate. I begged. I pleaded. I screamed. I cried. All the time I could see him through the opening nodding his head, saying, 'Not yet.'

"Then I knew there wasn't any hope. I would never make it. I was ready to give up. But the door opened, and he took me out and placed me on the shelf. One hour later he handed me a mirror and said, 'Look at yourself.' And I did. I said, 'That's not me; that couldn't be me. It's beautiful. I'm beautiful.'

" 'I want you to remember, then,' he said, 'I know it hurt to be rolled and patted, but if I just left you, you'd have dried up. I know it made you dizzy to spin around on the wheel, but if I had stopped, you would have crumbled. I know it hurt, and it was hot and disagreeable in the oven, but if I hadn't put you there, you would have cracked. I know the fumes were bad when I brushed and painted you all over, but if I hadn't done that, you never would have hardened. You would not have had any color in your life, and if I hadn't put you back in that second oven, you wouldn't survive for very long because the hardness would not have held. Now you are a finished product. You are what I had in mind when I first began with you.' "[27]

As grandparents, we will face many adversities in life. Trials that will attempt to split us apart—separate us from our children, our in-laws, our churches, and even our businesses. That's life! Some of us are in the oven screaming, hollering, kicking on the door, and yelling, "Let me out of here! I can't take it any longer!" Some of us are in the glaze stage and are getting our final paint job. The fumes and stench are bothering us and making our heads go in circles. A few of us are going round and round on the spinning wheel. We are disoriented and just want off. It's got to stop someday, so we figure it might as well be today.

Everything's a mess, and God keeps saying, "Not yet, not yet."

How much do you trust God with your life?

PRAYER

*F*ather God, Your Word tells me that You are with me in all of life's situations. My faith gives me the strength to believe this to be true. I praise You for giving me that assurance. Amen.

ACTION

Reconfirm your commitment to letting God do a good work in you.

TODAY'S WISDOM

Conduct is what we do; character is what we are. Conduct is the outward life; character is the life unseen, hidden within, yet evidenced by that which is seen. Conduct is external, seen from without; character is internal—operating within....Character is the state of the heart, conduct is its outward expression. Character is the root of the tree, conduct, the fruit it bears.

E.M. BOUNDS

From
Grammy's Kitchen

No-Cook Play Dough

> 2 teaspoons cooking oil
> 1 cup salt
> 1 ¼ cup water
> 2 tablespoons cornstarch
> 3 cups all-purpose flour
> food coloring

In a large bowl, mix cooking oil, salt, and water. Gradually add cornstarch and flour. Knead until smooth. Divide dough into parts and add food coloring. If the dough is too dry, add small amounts of water; if too sticky, add flour.

A Household Hint for the Kitchen

Take your empty Baggies from the market, fold lengthwise in fourths, and roll over a toilet paper tube, securing with a rubber band. They store neatly in a drawer and are ready to use anytime.

Petitions for
Our Grandchildren

❧❧❧

*You shall teach them diligently to your children
[and grandchildren], and shall talk of them when
you sit in your house, when you walk by the way,
when you lie down, and when you rise up.*

DEUTERONOMY 6:7 NKJV

$\mathcal{M}$OSES DIRECTED THE ISRAELI NATION to do everything possible to remember the commands (the sum and substance of the law) and to incorporate them into everyday life. Part of this included the spiritual education of the children. In Hebrew, the word for "parent" is teacher. As grandparents we become "grand teachers." Just because we aren't the parents doesn't mean we don't still have the responsibility to continue teaching when we are with our grandchildren. In the old days, spiritual teaching would take place daily through the study of God's Word, the reputation of the Law, and the examples the parents and grandparents exhibited in their lives. The instruction was more than just the reading and memorization of the law—it included the demonstration of a godly lifestyle woven into everyday living.

Today we need to be creative in the ways we teach. We should be alert to life and the events that are happening around us. Use the news to point out examples of good and evil. The seasonal holidays are great opportunities to evaluate the origins of each one. Anniversaries, birthdays, weddings, funerals, and new births are perfect times to instruct your children in God's laws. Strolling on the beach, hiking, sleeping out under the stars, cooking together, or working on a car can be treasured moments to teach truths.

As grandparents, we are always teaching—which is different than lecturing. Remain open to questions. Watch your nonverbal language when shocking comments come forth. Pray for wisdom, guidance, and patience before and during your times with your grandchildren.

ைஉஉஐ

PRAYER

*F*ather God, let me draw upon Your strength to be diligent in my teaching of Your Word to our youngsters. Give me creative ways I can use to transmit Your principles for life. Amen.

ACTION

*C*all your grandchildren today. In the conversations, share how God has been faithful to you recently. If you have a lot of grandchildren, you may want to spread your calls over several days.

TODAY'S WISDOM

*D*on't let what you cannot do interfere with what you can do.

JOHN WOODEN

A Penny Has Value

꧁꧂

Walk in a manner worthy of the God
who calls you into His own kingdom and glory.
1 Thessalonians 2:12

꧁꧂

THE FOLLOWING STORY WAS SENT TO ME by a friend. I don't know who the original author was, but I hope you'll find it as uplifting as I did!

꧁꧂

Several years ago, a friend of mine and her husband were invited to spend the weekend at the husband's employer's home. My friend, Arlene, was nervous about the weekend. The boss was very wealthy, with a fine home on the waterway and cars costing more than her house.

The first day and evening went well, and Arlene was delighted to have this rare glimpse into how the very wealthy live. The husband's employer was quite generous as a host, and took them to the finest restaurants. Arlene knew she would never have the opportunity to indulge in this kind of extravagance again, so she was enjoying herself immensely.

As the three of them were about to enter an exclusive restaurant that evening, the boss was walking slightly ahead of

Arlene and her husband. He stopped suddenly, looking down on the pavement for a long, silent moment.

Arlene wondered if she was supposed to pass him. There was nothing on the ground except a single darkened penny that someone had dropped and a few cigarette butts. Still silent, the man reached down and picked up the penny.

He held it up and smiled, and then put it into his pocket as if he had found a great treasure. How absurd! What need did this man have for a single penny? Why would he even take the time to stop and pick it up?

Throughout dinner, the entire scene nagged at her. Finally she could stand it no longer. She casually mentioned that her daughter once had a coin collection and asked if the penny he had found had been of some value.

A smile crept across the man's face as he reached into his pocket for the penny and held it out for her to see. She had seen many pennies before. What was the point of this?

"Look at it," he said. "Read what it says."

She read the words, "United States of America."

"No, not that. Read further."

"One cent?"

"No, keep reading."

"In God we trust?"

"Yes!"

"And?"

"And if I trust in God, the name of God is holy, even on a coin. Whenever I find a coin, I see that inscription. It is written on every single United States coin, but we never seem to notice it. God drops a message right in front of me telling me to trust Him? Who am I to pass it by? When I see a coin, I pray, I stop to see if my trust *is* in God at that moment. I pick the coin up as a response to God—that I do trust in Him. For a short time, at least, I cherish it as if it were gold.

I think it is God's way of starting a conversation with me. Lucky for me, God is patient and pennies are plentiful!"[28]

❧❧

Yes, we can trust in God. May our lives reveal this trust to our grandchildren. When they see us, do we reflect this assurance in our lifestyle? Remember, what they see us doing is more valuable than what they hear us saying.

❧❧

PRAYER

*F*ather God, let me be worthy to be called a child of Yours. Examine my heart and change it if it's not reflecting Your calling. Amen.

ACTION

*K*now that you are more worthy to God than a penny. You have worth—act upon this truth.

TODAY'S WISDOM

*W*e tend to believe that life will get better when, really, it just gets different. If the grass looks greener on the other side of your fence, it may be because you're not investing your time and energy in your own grass. Live in the present.

ELISA MORGAN AND CAROL KUYKENDALL

Memories of the Garden Bench

❧

I thank my God every time I remember you.

PHILIPPIANS 1:3 NIV

*I*T WAS A WARM SUNNY DAY for January in California. Two of our five grandchildren were helping us enjoy this fine day. Ten-and-a-half-year-old Christine was helping me, her "Grammy Em," plan and cook the dinner. She was picking flowers to arrange for our dinner table. "PaPa Bob" and Bevan were raking the garden and picking oranges, avocados, and lemons off the trees that surround our property.

As the afternoon progressed, our working men became warm and tired.

Christine said, "Grammy, let's have tea." That's all it takes for me to stop whatever I'm doing and put the kettle on. In the process of getting tea ready, we poured the men each a tall glass of fresh juice on ice and prepared some yummy-for-the-tummy snacks. We carried the treats up the hill to PaPa and Bevan. How happy they were to receive the refreshment! They thanked us and headed for the bench that sits under a large shady avocado tree overlooking the grounds and our quaint, tree-lined little Rumsey Drive that winds by our barn.

As Christine and I left them, we headed back toward the house. Christine took my hand and said, "Grammy, I love you."

"I love you, too, Christine," I said.

I prepared the teakettle, and Christine pulled down the teapot and put the teacups on the table with our special silver teaspoons. We toasted thick sourdough bread that we spread with jam and butter. It was an instant tea party—just Christine and me.

That night as my Bob and I crawled into bed, we began to share about our day with the oh-so-wonderful grandchildren.

"What do a PaPa and seven-year-old grandson talk about on the bench under the big avocado tree?" I asked.

"Oh, very special things," Bob replied. "Boys talk just like you girls talk."

I could still picture PaPa Bob and seven-year-old Bevan— with smudges of dirt on both their faces—sitting on that bench.

Bob continued, "I told Bevan, 'Someday, Bevan, when PaPa's in heaven and you drive down Rumsey Drive as a man, you'll look at this bench we are sitting on and you can remember the day that Grammy Em and sister Christine served us jam and toast with a glass of juice.' Then Bevan said, 'Not only will I remember, but I will bring my son and someday he will bring his son and point to the bench and tell him about the toast and jam we ate on the bench under that big avocado tree over there.'"

How does a little boy understand and think through the process of generations?

How blessed we are to have the God-given opportunity to teach our children and grandchildren about the beauty of God's creation, life and death, and most of all about God the Father, God the Son, and God the Holy Spirit.

ᗧᑫᗤ

PRAYER

*F*ather God, we think we only live for today, but Scripture tells us to look to the future and eternity. The world wants us to conform to the pressures of the here and now and focus on the temporal. Help me take time to develop a future orientation for myself and my family. What You have done for me in the past gives me hope for the future. Amen.

ACTION

• Take a grandchild's hand, and then take a walk and talk to each other.

• Give a cup of refreshment—a cup of tea or a glass of juice—to someone today.

• Tell someone, "I love you."

TODAY'S WISDOM

I urge you to live a life worthy of the calling you have received. Be completely humble and gentle; be patient, bearing with one another in love.

EPHESIANS 4:1-2 NIV

An Inheritance Challenge

❧

*A good man leaves an inheritance
to his children's children.*

PROVERBS 13:22

NOT TOO MANY YEARS AGO Bob and I were challenged to have a trust and will drawn up by our family attorney who specializes in these areas. We knew that because of the way our taxes are structured, if something would happen to one of us, our estate would be locked up in a mountain of laws and regulations if we didn't have a will made.

As we were deciding on how our estate would be divided, this particular verse of Scripture challenged us to leave part of our worldly possessions to our five grandchildren. Not only were they listed as beneficiaries, but we set up a California Gift of Minors trust fund for each of them with our stockbroker. Each birthday and each Christmas we contribute so much money to each account. On their eighteenth birthdays the stocks and bonds become theirs to be used for their college education.

In the process, they are learning about mutual funds and the stock market. What a delight to see them take an interest in financial matters!

❧❦❧

PRAYER

*F*ather God, thank You for giving me an abundance so I am able to share my blessings with my grandchildren. Amen.

ACTION

*M*ake a will that includes your grandchildren in your inheritance.

TODAY'S WISDOM

If you believe in something, you support it. If you support something, the time comes when good wishes and cordial words are not enough and your hand reaches for your pocketbook. Then the fun begins. For giving is fun. If you refuse to give, your support is wavering; and if your support wavers, it can't be that you believe in that something in any strong way. Maybe our account books, after all, offer the honest list of those things in which we really believe.

KENNETH IRVING BROWN

SPIRIT LIFTERS

♥ For an investment in the future, plant a tree! If you don't have a yard, think about making a "green" donation to your church grounds or even to a local school.

♥ On a slow afternoon, put on soft music and browse through your favorite recipe book for ideas and inspiration.

♥ Frame a card with your favorite Scripture verse and hang the picture next to your desk or kitchen sink. When you need a break, ponder it.

Helping
Others Win

❧❧

I will lift up my eyes to the mountains;
from where shall my help come?
My help comes from the LORD.
PSALM 121:1-2

A FEW YEARS AGO, at the Seattle Special Olympics, nine contestants, all physically or mentally disabled, assembled at the
starting line for the 100-yard dash. At the gun, they all started
out, not exactly in a dash, but with a relish to run the race to
the finish and win.

All, that is, except one little boy who stumbled on the
asphalt, tumbled over a couple of times, and began to cry.
The other contestants heard the boy cry. A few slowed down
and looked back. Then a couple people turned around and
went back.

One girl with Down's Syndrome bent down and kissed
him and said, "This will make it better." Then the contestants
left behind linked arms and walked together to the finish line.
Everyone in the stadium stood and the cheering went on for
several minutes. People who were there are still telling the
story. Why? Because deep down we know this one thing:
What matters in this life is more than winning for ourselves.

What matters in this life is helping others win, even if it means slowing down and changing our course.[29]

❧❧

What a wonderful story to illustrate how we, the healthy, should get the same perspective as these children have in life. We are not always called to win the race; often we are to help others win the race.

Most of us as grandparents have already run most of the race of life. In some cases, we are winners. Some of us didn't finish the race as we would have liked. And some of us are still running the race. No matter where we are in life's race, we now have the opportunity to help our grandchildren run their courses.

Life will be more difficult for those coming behind than during our days. Each of us has a different calling on how we will help. Rich or poor, we can offer much to these youngsters through our life wisdom, God's Word, and our various resources.

❧❧

PRAYER

*F*ather God, help me examine my life to figure out how I am going to help my grandchildren run the race called life. May I be an encouragement in all that I do. Amen.

ACTION

Create a plan to help your grandchildren be winners.

TODAY'S WISDOM

A candle loses nothing by lighting another candle.

Know the Bent of
Your Grandchild

✥

Train a child in the way he should go,
and when he is old he will not turn from it.
PROVERBS 22:6 NIV

As I THINK ABOUT OUR CHILDREN, Brad and Jenny, and look
into the various shades of color in the eyes of our grandchildren—Christine, Chad, Bevan, Bradley Joe II, and Weston—
I see seven unique people. How am I ever going to understand
the uniqueness of each of these children? I know that I have
to attempt to understand each of them if I am going to have
an impact upon molding healthy, godly character in their lives.
At the heart of each child is a cry, "Please take time to know
me. I am different from anyone else. My sensitivities, my likes,
dislikes, tenderness of heart are different from my brothers and
sisters."

In raising our own children, we saw so many differences
between Jenny and Brad. Even as adults they are still different.
I, in God's wisdom, had to realize that my approach to moti-
vating them had to be styled differently for each of them.
Children want to be trained in a personal and tailor-made
way.

In our key verse for today, we first see the word "train." In the Hebrew, this word originally referred to the palate (the roof of the mouth) and to the gums. In Bible times, the midwife would stick her fingers into a sweet substance and place her fingers into the new child's mouth, creating a sucking desire in the child. The child would then be delicately given to the mother, whereby the child would start nursing. This was the earliest form of "training." The child mentioned in Proverbs 22:6 can fall between a newborn and a person that is of marrying age.

The second part of this verse is "when he is old he will not turn from it." At first I thought this meant an older person who had become wayward yet finally returned to the Lord. Little did I know that this word "old" meant "bearded" or "chin." Solomon is talking about a young man who begins to grow a beard when he approaches maturity. For some it might be in junior high school and for others it might be college. The concept is that we as parents are charged to continue training our children as long as they are under our care.

Note that we are to train a child in *his* way—not our way, our plan, our idea. It's important to see that the verse is not a guarantee to parents that raising a child in God's way means he will return back again when he is old. I honestly don't believe this is the proper principle for us as parents. When we train our children according to "his way"—the child's way—we approach each child differently. We don't compare them one to another. Each child is uniquely made.

When I became a student of my two children, I began to design different approaches for each child. Jenny was not Brad, and Brad certainly wasn't Jenny. Each child has his or her own bent and is already established when God places him or her in our family. God has given you unique grandchildren. Get to know them.

ഇൗഉൗ

PRAYER

*F*ather God, You know how much I want to know the bent of my grandchildren. Give me the godly wisdom to understand who they are and to be an encouragement to them. Help me to build them up to be all that You designed them to be. Amen.

ACTION

• Write down in your journal the ways your grandchildren are different.

• Think about how you will train them based on these differences.

• Learn one new thing about each of your grandchildren today. Do something with that information.

• Praise your grandchild today for being uniquely made.[30]

TODAY'S WISDOM

*W*hen your grandchildren are young you talk to them about Jesus—when they are old you talk to Jesus about them.

Your Days
Are Numbered

*It is appointed for men to die once
and after this comes judgment.*

HEBREWS 9:27

*I*F WE JUST HAD ONE YEAR TO LIVE, what would we do? This is
a great question, and one we should think through. In fact, at
some point in time we will not have the luxury of living one
year because of a terminal illness or even a sudden death by
natural causes. A.W. Tozer wrote a response to this basic question of life. See if your thoughts might be similar to his.

Suppose that I were to learn that I had just one year to
live—the number of my days was to be only 365. What
should I do with the precious few days that remained to me?

The first thing is that I would have to arrive at some plan
of action in conformity with known facts. I mean the facts of
life and death and what God has to say about them in the
Bible. However much I might ignore them while the hope of
long life lay before me, with that hope shrunk to a brief year,

170

these facts would take on tremendous proportions. With death stalking me, I would have little interest in trivial subjects and would instead be concerned with the essentials.

I would stop hoping vaguely that somehow things would come out all right, and I would get down to realities. After all, the Bible says, "We are all as an unclean thing, and all our righteousnesses are as filthy rags" (Isaiah 64:6). And "for whosoever shall keep the whole law, and yet offend in one point, he is guilty of all" (James 2:10). Knowing that "it is appointed unto men once to die, but after this the judgment" (Hebrews 9:27), I would take no rest until I had absolute assurance on these vital matters.

I would come to God on His own terms. It was Jesus who said, "I am the way, the truth, and the life; no man cometh unto the Father but by me" (John 14:6). I would not stand on ceremony nor allow myself to be hindered by the niceties of religion. For the Bible says, "Not by works of righteousness which we have done, but according to [God's] mercy he saved us" (Titus 3:5).

I would want to *know* that my sins were forgiven, that I had passed from death unto life, and that Jesus Christ was my personal Savior. "Neither is there salvation in any other; for there is no other name under heaven given among men whereby we must be saved" (Acts 4:12).

The Bible goes on to say, "Christ also hath once suffered for sins, the just for the unjust, that He might bring us to God" (1 Peter 3:18). He "was delivered [up to death] for our offenses, and was raised again for our justification" (Romans 4:25).

I would put away apathy, come boldly to Christ, and throw myself at His feet: "Believe on the Lord Jesus Christ, and thou shalt be saved." The Bible says, "For God so loved the world that he gave his only begotten Son, that whosoever believeth in him should not perish but have everlasting life" (Acts 16:31; John 3:16). I would come believing that God's promise of forgiveness and eternal life includes me.

Then, a new person in Christ, I would give the last remaining year to God. All the wreckage and loss of the years behind me would spur me on to make the one year before me a God-blessed success.

Now all this would seem to me to be the good and right thing to do for one who had just a year to live. But since we do not know whether we have a year before us, or a day or 10 days, and since what would be right for the last year would be right for the whole life—even if its years were many—then the conclusion is plain. Our cry to God should be, "Teach us to number our days, that we may apply our hearts to wisdom" (Psalm 90:12).

I do not know what others may want to do, but I want to get down to business and live as if this year were my last. Then, if God should spare me to a ripe old age, I can depart without regrets.

If *you* had just one year to live, what would *you* do?[31]

∽♈ॐ

PRAYER

*F*ather God, teach me to number my days and to live each day, week, month, and year as if it were my last. Reconfirm my purpose in life. Let me not waste my time serving just myself. Challenge me today in a new way. Amen.

ACTION

*W*rite in your journal what you would do if you had just one year to live. Discuss this with your mate.

TODAY'S WISDOM

*T*ell God all that is in your heart, as one unloads one's heart to a dear friend. People who have no secrets from each other never want for subjects of conversation: They do not weigh their words because there is nothing to be kept back. Neither do they seek for something to say; they talk out of the abundance of their hearts, just what they think. Blessed are they who attain to such familiar, unreserved intercourse with God.

FRANÇOIS DE LA MOTHE FÉNELON

A Grandparent
or a Friend?

*I will walk within my house
in the integrity of my heart.*

PSALM 101:2

*I*N GEORGE WASHINGTON'S DAY, two candidates applied for a certain office. One was a warm friend and lifelong associate of Washington; the other, decidedly hostile to the politics of Washington, arrayed himself in the ranks of the opposition. It was supposed that Washington would decide for his friend; but, to the surprise of all, the other person was appointed to office.

Upon being remonstrated, Washington replied, "My friend I receive with a cordial welcome to my house and welcome to my heart; but, with all his good qualities, he is not a man of business. His opponent is, with all his hostility to me, a man of business. My private feelings have nothing to do in this case: I am not George Washington, but president of the United States. As George Washington, I would do this man any kindness in my power; but, as president, I can do nothing."

What a great example of integrity! As grandparents we must step back and objectively evaluate positions. As Bob and I observe changes in our social structure, we see that too many parents and grandparents consider their children friends. When this happens, they lose a key parental role by making decisions based on friendship rather than good parenting.

We are to be friendly and just, but, above all, we must have integrity.[32]

PRAYER

*F*ather God, help me make the tough decisions of life without compromising my status as a loving grandparent. I want to be strong in my position. Even though there is a fine line between tough and tender, I truly want to be a woman of character. Amen.

ACTION

*S*tep up to the plate and be a friendly grandparent.

TODAY'S WISDOM

*Y*ou will find as you look back upon life that the moments when you have really lived are the moments when you have done things in the spirit of love.

HENRY DRUMMOND

From
Grammy's Kitchen

S'mores

Ingredients

> 12 graham cracker squares
> 12 marshmallows
> 12 squares of Hershey chocolate candy
> plenty of napkins
> wire coat hangers to roast marshmallows

Procedure

1. Straighten out the wire coat hangers.

2. Place 1 to 2 marshmallows on one end of the wire hanger.

3. Place marshmallow over the heat source and rotate. Leave until the marshmallow begins to cook.

4. When marshmallow is light brown, remove from heat source.

5. Take 1 graham cracker square and lay a Hershey chocolate square on top of cracker.

6. Place roasted marshmallow on top of Hershey bar.

7. Take another graham cracker square and place on top of the marshmallow.

8. You now have a sandwich—press the two graham cracker squares together until the marshmallow and chocolate blend together.

You now have a s'more for eating—and it is so good!

Caution: Use safety precautions with young children around heat source.

A Household Hint for the Kitchen

Make up your own TV dinners. Use containers purchased in your market for microwave or regular ovens. Put your leftovers in sections of the trays and freeze. Great for PaPa's dinner when Grammy's away.

Have a "No Shoulds" Day

❦❦❦

The righteous shall flourish like a palm tree; he shall grow like a cedar in Lebanon. Those who are planted in the house of the LORD shall flourish in the courts of our God. They shall still bear fruit in old age; they shall be fresh and flourishing.

PSALM 92:12-14 NKJV

WHEN THE GRANDCHILDREN COME TO VISIT their grandparents for the night or just the waking hours of light, they are usually tired. They have been on a hectic schedule all week with school, sports, music lessons, and homework. They would just as soon kick back and get caught up with sleep. On occasion, plan a "No Shoulds Day." This is a time when nothing is planned: No zoo trips, no Disneyland journey, no movie outings, no special activities. Let the grandkids do exactly what they would like to do...and that's usually rest. This is a time to get caught up, to rest, to dream, to read a good book, to listen to good music. No expectations and no responsibilities. As the kids say, "Just veg out."

Ideas for a "No Shoulds Day"

- Do whatever you want to do: sleep late, wear your PJs around the house all day. Don't comb your hair or even brush your teeth.

- You can have no meals or you can have five meals.

Have dinner for breakfast, and breakfast for dinner. Use only paper products—no dishwashing allowed.

• Watching birds fly and chirp in the yard is permissible. Even tracking a bug crawling over decaying plants is okay.

• Be sure to plan the next "No Shoulds Day" before the grandchildren go back home to their demanding routines.

୨୦୬୭

PRAYER

*F*ather God, I must remember that grandchildren have often been indulged all week and that they would just as soon not have to be entertained. Often they just want to be with me. Let me learn to keep it simple. Amen.

ACTION

*P*lan a "No Shoulds Day" with your grandchildren.

TODAY'S WISDOM

*W*ith the fearful strain that is on me day and night, if I did not laugh, I should die.

ABRAHAM LINCOLN

The Refiner

And I will bring [them] through the fire,
refine them as silver is refined, and test them as gold is tested.
They will call on My name, and I will answer them.

ZECHARIAH 13:9

Gᴏᴅ ᴏꜰᴛᴇɴ ᴜꜱᴇꜱ ꜱᴜꜰꜰᴇʀɪɴɢ. My friends Glen and Marilyn
Heavilin, for instance, know the kind of suffering Job knew.
They have lost three sons—one in crib death; one twin by
pneumonia; and the second twin by a teenage drunk driver.
Glen and Marilyn were tested, but they have come through
the refiner's fire. Today they use their experiences to glorify the
name of the Lord.

Marilyn has written *Roses in December,* which is the story
of how they lost their sons. She has had the opportunity to
speak all over the country in high school auditoriums filled
with teenagers. There she shares her story and talks about life
and death, chemical dependency, and God.

Did God know what He was doing when He chose the
Heavilins? Of course. They have come forth as gold fired in the
heat of life, and they are able to shine for Him. Their pain will
never be gone, but they still minister. They've been very active
in "Compassionate Friends," a support group for families who
have experienced the death of children. God knew the path the

Heavilins would take when they faced their tragic losses, and He's been there as their faith in Him has been purified.

Every one of us has experienced some kind of tragedy. It's not the specifics of the event that matter as much as how we handle it. Whatever loss you're dealing with and however you're being tested, you can be sure that others have been tested that way too. So don't go through the testing alone. Trust in God, and find someone you can trust who will bear the burden with you. You, too, can and will come forth as gold.

Remember that Jesus knows your pain, and He is always with you to help you get through the tough times in life. Trust Him now. It's all part of the "coming forth as gold" that Job talks about.[33]

❧❧❧

PRAYER

*F*ather God, sometimes it hurts so much to go through trials, but I know I will come out stronger. Help me remember You are with me. Amen.

ACTION

*T*hink about how God might be using this pain and suffering in your life to help your Christian growth, to help you "come forth as gold."

TODAY'S WISDOM

*I*t's not hard to make decisions when you know what your values are.

ROY DISNEY

A Mirror of Jesus

For you have been called for this purpose,
since Christ also suffered for you, leaving you
an example for you to follow in His steps.

1 PETER 2:21

*W*HAT A CHALLENGE FOR US AS GRANDPARENTS to follow in Jesus'
steps! That's what today's verse tells us to do. Many years ago
I read a book entitled *In His Steps*. It was the story of a man
who, for a period of time, attempted to walk in the steps of
Jesus. Everything he said, everywhere he went, all decisions he
made were done as if he were Jesus. As you can imagine, it was
just about impossible. However, the experience changed this
man's life forever.

We are not Jesus—nor will we ever be. Yet Jesus left us with
His example of a godly life. As we walk through life on earth
we will experience daily situations that will reveal our character. Jesus gives us the example of kindness and gentleness.
He was full of sympathy and affection and always loved with
mercy.

Jesus essentially said, "Beloved, I understand your pain,
your grief, the tragedy of friends who betray you. I know you
live in a world where others have sickness and sin you can do
nothing about. I care and I can help you. I can cleanse you

and heal you today." As the Lord lives in you, He will form you into the beautiful, marvelous image of God according to your own uniqueness.

No, we can't be Jesus. But we can develop a teachable spirit. We can love Him and desire Him in our hearts with all our soul, mind, spirit, and strength. We will then find ourselves transformed into a giving, loving person with the joy of Jesus in our hearts. Our character will then reveal the likeness of Jesus. Our spirits will help the helpless, pray for the sick, feed and clothe the homeless, and support those whom God lifts up to be missionaries where we can't go.

You may be the only Christian influence your grandchildren might have. You will reflect the character of God to these young impressionable treasures. They will catch more often who you are rather than what you say. Their eyes are like a lighthouse beam always searching the dark night.

As grandparents may we walk in Jesus' steps as we follow His call for us today. There is no greater calling than to be godly grandparents who let Jesus' love pass through our lives and into our grandchildren.

ॐॐ

PRAYER

Father God, I am challenged to walk in Your steps. Reveal to me what I should do to be a loving and caring grandparent. I want Your vision to be mine. Amen.

ACTION

Ask yourself, "Are the qualities of Jesus evident in my life?"

TODAY'S WISDOM

Words are more powerful than perhaps anyone suspects, and once deeply engraved in a child's mind, they are not easily eradicated.

MAY SARTON

The Lost Mitt

❧❧❧

And the LORD *will continually guide you, and satisfy your desire in scorched places, and give strength to your bones; and you will be like…a spring of water whose waters do not fail.*

ISAIAH 58:11

*I*T WAS BRAD'S FIRST REAL-LEATHER baseball mitt. Bob taught him how to break it in with special oil. The oil is rubbed into the pocket of the glove, then Brad tossed his baseball from hand to hand to form a pocket just right for him. Brad loved his mitt and worked for hours each day to make it fit him just right. He was so happy to have such a special glove for his baseball practices and games.

One afternoon after practice, one of the older boys asked to see his mitt. He looked it over, then threw it into a grassy field. Brad ran to find his special possession, but he couldn't locate it. Nowhere was his mitt to be found. With a frightened, hurt heart, Brad came home in tears.

After he told me the story, I encouraged him by saying it had to be there somewhere. "I'll go with you Brad, and we'll search the lot until we find it."

"But, Mom, I did search the lot, and it's not there," replied Brad tearfully.

Bob said, "Brad, let's pray and ask God to help us." By now

it was beginning to get dark and we needed to hurry, so into the car we jumped. As Bob drove Brad and me to the baseball field, we asked God to please guide our steps directly to the glove. Parking quickly, we headed for the field. Again we asked God to point us in the right direction. Immediately Brad ran into the tall grass of the field and there, about 20 feet away, "thumb up," was Brad's glove.

God answers our prayers! Sometimes it's wait, yes, or later. For Brad, that day it was yes. God said in essence, "I'll direct you to find the mitt of this young boy whose heart was broken because of a bully kid and a lost glove."

Do you have a "lost glove" today? Go before God and praise Him for the promise He gave us in today's verse. If God says it, believe it. He *will* direct you and guide you. Open your heart to listen to what His direction is, then press ahead. The grass may seem too tall to see very far, but trust the Lord and keep walking until you feel in your heart the peace you desire. God may lead in a direction you least expect, but step forward with confidence in the Lord.[34]

PRAYER

*F*ather God, help me walk in the field of grass, letting You continually guide me. Amen.

ACTION

*S*tep out in faith that you will find your "lost glove."

TODAY'S WISDOM

*K*eep away from people who try to belittle your ambitions. Small people always do that, but the really great make you feel that you, too, can become great.

MARK TWAIN

Spirit Lifters

♥ God has good plans for us today that give us both a future and a hope (Jeremiah 29:11).

♥ God is the blessed controller of all things today (1 Timothy 6:15).

♥ We are foreordained to be molded into the image of His Son, Jesus, today (Romans 8:29).

♥ We can do all things through Christ who strengthens us today (Philippians 4:13).

♥ We are responsible to bear much fruit today, and thereby glorify the Father (John 15:8).

♥ Nothing can separate us from the love of Christ today (Romans 8:35,38-39).

♥ God is the love of our lives, and He has called us in accordance with His purpose; therefore, He has promised us that all things will work together today for our good (Romans 8:28).

♥ God loves us with an everlasting love today (Jeremiah 31:3).

Finding Favor
in God's Eyes

ஐ௨௨

Noah found favor in the eyes of the LORD...Noah did;
according to all that God had commanded him.
GENESIS 6:8,22

ONE WAY TO FIND FAVOR WITH GOD is to love His little children. In the New Testament, we read where Jesus loved the young children and warned us as adults to be careful not to harm the little children. As a grandparent, I can gain favor with God by being kind and gentle with the little ones in my family. What an honor to be a part of the spiritual development of our grandchildren!

Being a person who stays on top of the current events of our day, I learn about people who are honored by the world. In government, sports, business, medicine, education, theater, and music, all have personalities who rise to the top of their profession and are honored. They are nominated to be in high office, a member of the World Series team, a discoverer of a new cancer drug, the teacher of the year, an Oscar winner, or the most beautiful tenor the world has ever heard. On and on we go. Man finding favor with man.

Have you ever thought how much richer it would be to have God find favor with you as a grandparent? I stand in awe when I think of God finding favor in me—and He does! But only through His marvelous grace are we able to come to Him face-to-face.

Noah lived in a world much like today—a world full of sin. Man hasn't changed much over the centuries; we just give sin a different name. Yet through all this wickedness, Noah lived a godly life. His life was pleasing to God. But Noah didn't find favor because of his individual goodness. He found it through his personal faith in God. We are also judged according to the same standard—that of our personal faith and obedience. Even though Noah was upright and blameless before God, he wasn't perfect. God recognized that Noah's life reflected a genuine faith, not always a perfect faith.

Do you sometimes feel all alone in your walk with God? I know I do. Noah found that it wasn't the surroundings of his life that kept him in close fellowship with God, but it was the heart of Noah that qualified him to find friendship with God.

As a grandma, I get excited about the arrival of the grandchildren. I realize they are the future. They are the legacy of the Barnes' family tree, and my heart softens as they give me a big hug and are so excited to be with me. It isn't important to find favor from our fellow man. God's favor is so much more rewarding. Somehow some of God's favor to me is passed down through me to my grandchildren. God gives us grace to live victoriously: "He gives more grace" (James 4:6).

PRAYER

Father God, let my eyes always be upon You and not on the applause of my fellow man. That honor will someday pass away, but Your honor is eternal. Thank You for honoring me through my grandchildren. Amen.

ACTION

Call one or more of your grandchildren today and express your love for them.

TODAY'S WISDOM

The world is a looking-glass, and gives back to every man the reflection of his own face. Frown at it, and it in turn will look sourly at you, laugh at it, and with it, and it's a jolly, kind companion.

WILLIAM MAKEPEACE THACKERAY

A Formula for Life

❧❧❧

*Seek first His kingdom and His righteousness,
and all these things will be added to you.*
MATTHEW 6:33

$\mathcal{W}$E LIVE IN A VERY ANXIOUS SOCIETY. Many of us are more worried about tomorrow than today. We bypass all of today's contentment because of what might happen tomorrow. In Matthew 6:31, we read that the early Christians asked the same basic questions we do:

• What will we eat?
• What will we drink?
• What will we wear?

Jesus tells them in verse 34, "Do not worry about tomorrow; for tomorrow will care for itself. Each day has enough trouble of its own." The formula Jesus gives for establishing the right priorities of life is in today's verse. Bob and I have used this verse as our mission verse for the last 42 years. Each day we claim these two instructions:

• seek *His* kingdom
• seek *His* righteousness

Often we are overwhelmed by having too many things to do. Life offers many good choices on how to schedule our time. But we all have only 24 hours in a day. How are we to use these hours effectively? When we seek these two items first—God's kingdom then His righteousness—we find that our day takes shape, and we can say "yes" we will do that or "no" we will not do that. We determine what is important and what isn't, and how much time we are willing to give each activity. The Bible gives us guidelines for priorities:

- our personal relationships with Him (Matthew 6:33; Philippians 3:8)

- our time for home and family (Genesis 2:24; Psalm 127:3; 1 Timothy 3:2-5)

- our time for work (1 Thessalonians 4:11-12)

- our time for ministry and community activities (Colossians 3:17).

We cannot do all the things that come our way. Bob and I have a saying that helps us when we have too many choices: "Say no to the good things; say yes for the best." So don't be afraid to say "no." If you have established Matthew 6:33 as one of the key verses in your life, you can very quickly decide whether a particular opportunity will help you seek God's kingdom and seek His righteousness.

After learning to say "no" easily, you can begin to major on the big things of life and not get bogged down by minor issues or situations.[35]

꿁ꙴꙴ

PRAYER

*F*ather God, I fell so rushed in my daily scheduling. I look to Your wisdom to help me establish my priorities. Help me say no when I'm overcommitted. Amen.

ACTION

*L*ook in the mirror, pucker your lips, breathe through your mouth, and say, "No! No! No!" That wasn't so hard, was it?

TODAY'S WISDOM

*P*eople who want to move mountains must start by carrying small stones.

AUTHOR UNKNOWN

You're Never
Too Old

❧❧

Be hospitable to one another without complaint.

1 PETER 4:9

Y OU'RE NEVER TOO OLD TO OFFER HOSPITALITY to your guests.
As a grandparent, I find plenty of opportunity to open my
front door to various ages of people. One of my fondest
memories is when my five grandchildren come to visit. What
a delight to host them! We usually end up in the kitchen
making one of my favorite treats. Flour appears on the
kitchen floor, dishes get dirty, milk sometimes gets spilled,
but all-in-all it's a great day.

I learned a lot about hospitality from my own mother. My
mother, at 77, lived in a one-room efficiency apartment on the
fifteenth floor of a senior citizen building. She continually
shared hospitality with a cup of tea, a cookie, a piece of carrot
cake or banana bread. Her guests always felt special sipping tea
in a real china teacup, eating cookies placed on a pretty plate
with a paper doily, and enjoying a few flowers on the table
with a lit candle.

Do you grumble at the thought of inviting guests into
your home? Many of today's women seem to avoid hospitality

due to the pressure of their busy lives. But it didn't take much for Mama to be hospitable. One cup of tea, one cookie. Hospitality is the act of caring for one another. We can entertain all we like, but not until we care does it become hospitality.

So many times we feel things have to be perfect—the right time, a clean house, the right food. Yet today's Scripture tells us to cheerfully share our homes. When was the last time you had guests over?

Some people have a gift of serving others through hospitality, but I've found one thing to be true: Hospitality can be taught. Also, the more you entertain, the easier it becomes. Some of the best times in our home have been the simplest.

One very busy working mom discovered the way to fast, convenient hospitality. On her way home from work she picked up a bunch of flowers, a frozen lasagna from the supermarket, which she threw in her own casserole dish, and a frozen cake. She tossed a prepared salad in her wooden bowl, got out the cake for dessert, and lit a candle. Within moments she served a lovely dinner to guests who later helped clean up the kitchen, exclaiming, "This has been a delightfully delicious evening."

No one knew she didn't work hours preparing the meal. We can do whatever we want to do however we want to do it!

First Peter 4:11 says that if anyone serves he should do it with the strength God provides. God will provide the strength as we provide the desire. Jesus often fed people before He preached. Having friends in our home gives us the opportunity to let them see Jesus in us, to feel our spirits, to be touched by our love and caring. Many doors have been opened in the hearts of our friends when we've shared a meal together.[36]

Welcome the single widow or widower down the street to

come for a cup of tea in the afternoon. It will be an experience he or she will never forget. You'll be a shining example
in the neighborhood when you reach out and extend a warm
welcome to someone who needs a little comfort food.

❧

PRAYER

*F*ather God, thank You for giving me the gift of
hospitality. I so enjoy having people in my home.
The joy I receive when the grandchildren drop by is
so delightful. It just makes my day. Amen.

ACTION

*I*nvite someone over for a cup of tea with a bit of
sweets.

TODAY'S WISDOM

'Mid pleasures and palaces
Though we may roam,
Be it ever so humble,
There's no place like home.

AUTHOR UNKNOWN

From
Grammy's Kitchen

No Grill Sandwich

1 serving

> 2 bacon slices
> 2 bread slices (toasted)
> mayonnaise or 1000 Island dressing
> 2 slices lunch meat (your choice)
> prewashed lettuce
> 2 tomato slices

Heat bacon in a microwave according to package instructions. Spread mayonnaise on two slices of toasted bread. Top one slice with lunch meat and lettuce. Top other with bacon slices and tomato. Stack one slice of bread on the other. Cut into triangles.

Keep Climbing
the Mountain

☙❧

My help is from Jehovah who made the mountains!
And the heavens too!

PSALM 121:1 TLB

*A*s I WALKED THROUGH MY cancer treatment, I often wondered if I was going to make it. Yes, my support group encouraged me. Hundreds and hundreds of prayer partners assured me by cards and letters that I was going to make it. My mind, however, was sometimes plagued with negative thoughts about my future. Satan so wanted to defeat me by making me lose hope for recovery. Yet my faith remained victorious, and my daily walk with God helped me climb the many mountains put before me.

Bill Martin Jr. tells a story of how a young Indian boy was able to overcome his fear of failure.

> "Grandfather, will I ever be strong like you?" the little boy asked.
>
> His grandfather reassured him, "You're growing stronger every day."
>
> "How strong must I be, Grandfather?" the boy asked.
>
> "You must be so strong that you will not speak with anger even when your heart is filled with

anger....You must be so strong that you will listen to what others are saying even when your own thoughts are begging for expression....You must be so strong that you will always stop to remember what happened yesterday and foresee what will happen tomorrow so that you will know what to do today."

"Then will I be strong enough to cross over the dark mountains?" the boy asked.

The wise grandfather answered, "You already have crossed some of the dark mountains, my grandson. But these mountains of sorrow have no beginning and no ending. They are all around us. We can only know that we are crossing them when we want to be weak but choose to be strong."[37]

When you're called to cross the dark mountains surrounding you, be brave even when you feel weak. Lift your face skyward and pray that God will give you strength far beyond your expectations.

PRAYER

*F*ather God, today I am weak. I need your strength. Encourage me so I can continue going on. Help me face the unknown knowing that You know everything. Amen.

ACTION

*T*ake one step at a time. Move forward.

TODAY'S WISDOM

O my people, trust him all the time. Pour out your longings before him, for he can help!

PSALM 62:8 TLB

Being a Helpmate

It is not good for the man to be alone;
I will make him a helper suitable for him.

GENESIS 2:18

ONE OF THE GREAT JOYS OF BEING an older woman is to help teach the younger women how to be helpers for their husbands. Granddaughters need to know your wisdom when it comes to relationships of marriage. This is one of the joys of being an older woman.

A pastor while meeting an irreligious lady whose husband was trying to serve God addressed her, "Madam, I think your husband is looking upwards, making some effort to rise above the world toward God and heaven. You must not let him try alone. Whenever I see the husband struggling alone in such efforts, it makes me think of a dove endeavoring to fly upwards while it has one broken wing. It leaps and flutters, and perhaps rises a little way; and then it becomes wearied, and drops back again to the ground. If both wings cooperate then it mounts easily and reaches to the highest, but it needs some help in order to gain its fullest potential."

Being a helper to your husband is one of the great principles of marriage. What a difference it would make if more women would uphold their husbands as they attempt to rise above the world toward God and heaven! You can be the facilitator who will help women understand and implement Paul's teaching in Titus 2:3-5. "Older women...[are to] encourage the young women to love their husbands, to love their children, to be sensible, pure, workers at home, kind, being subject to their own husbands, so that the word of God may not be dishonored."

As a grandparent the easiest way to teach is by example. Often the children who are married are not always eager to ask their parents about marriage, but they cannot deny you living and modeling Scripture. Be available to help when it is requested. We must be sensitive that we don't barge in unannounced into their lives, but be prepared when the time comes.

PRAYER

*F*ather God, You know how I, as a mature woman of God, want to be used in encouraging younger women how to be makers of their homes. Give me the perfect timing to be available. In the meantime, I will demonstrate Your Scripture by my life. Amen.

ACTION

*T*ell your husband how much you love him.

TODAY'S WISDOM

*E*ternity is not something that begins after you are dead. It is going on all the time. We are in it now.

CHARLOTTE PERKINS GILMAN

They Are Watching

❦❦❦

So take a new grip with your tired hands,
stand firm on your shaky legs, and mark out a straight,
smooth path for your feet so that those who
follow you, though weak and lame, will not fall
and hurt themselves but become strong.

HEBREWS 12:12-13 TLB

*I*LLNESS OFTEN CHANGES OUR APPEARANCE. I guess being bald is common to those patients who have had heavy dosages of chemotherapy. During my cancer treatment I faced this reality. As my hair started to fall out in the shower and on my pillowcase, I wondered, *How can I turn this lemon into lemonade?* I decided to have a "haircut party" with my family.

As we gathered that day on the patio, my son, Brad, brought his razor that he uses on the boys for their summer butch haircuts, and he gave me a buzz cut. The children and grandchildren were all gathered around to observe and to take a few historic pictures. I looked so cute that all the men and boys decided they wanted a buzz cut so they could be just like Grammy. However our daughter, Jenny, said, "Mom, I love you a whole lot, but I'm not going to get a crew cut." I didn't blame her a bit. This was one of my fond memories of a bad occasion. Everyone was watching to see how I would react. My reaction set the tone for them—I modeled joy for them in a difficult situation. They were watching me![38]

∽℘℘∾

PRAYER

*F*ather God, Satan meant it for evil, but you intended it for good. You truly helped me take a negative and make it into a positive. Thank You for Your creativity. Amen.

ACTION

*M*ake lemonade out of a lemon in your life.

TODAY'S WISDOM

*H*ow far you go in life depends on your being tender with the young, compassionate with the aged, sympathetic with the striving, and tolerant of the weak and the strong. Because someday in life you will have been all of these.

GEORGE WASHINGTON CARVER

Praying Grandparents

Confess your sins to one another, and pray for one another so that you may be healed. The effective prayer of a righteous man can accomplish much.

JAMES 5:16

*P*RAYER BUILDS A HEDGE AROUND those you pray for. Without this protection, those we love go out into the world vulnerable. We are to be watchful (Colossians 4:2). This mean there is something out there to beware of. If we aren't aware of danger, it might very easily engulf us and harm us.

Prayer also gives us a thankful heart for all the things the Lord gives us. As grandparents, become devoted in prayer for your grandchildren, no matter how young they are. Also, be earnest to uphold their parents in prayer. We can't tell you how often God has answered our prayer requests regarding our children and grandchildren.

Campus Crusade, through their radio ministry "Family Life Today," gives us grandparents seven tips for prayer:

1. That God would place a protective hedge around our grandchildren so strong that Satan cannot enter and lead them into temptation (Psalm 33:20; James 5:8).

2. That grandchildren would use godly wisdom in selecting their friends, for friends and peers do make a difference (Proverbs 1:10; Deuteronomy 13:6,8). Ask God to give them a discernment of people as well as knowing the difference between right and wrong.

3. That our grandchildren would stay pure (Psalm 24:4; Job 17:9).

4. That they will be caught if they wander into cheating, lies, or mischief (Proverbs 20:30).

5. That they will be alert and thinking clearly as they attend school and take exams, and they will be motivated to do the best they are capable of doing (Ephesians 4:1).

6. For the parents that their children will one day marry; that they will come from godly homes and will have an appetite for spiritual truth; that their goals and purposes will be the same as those of your own children, and that their future homes would be characterized by Deuteronomy 5:29: "They [would have] such a heart in them that they would fear Me and keep all My commandments always" (NASB).

7. That our grandchildren's lives will count for God and that He will use them as a testimony and witness for His glory. Ask that they exceed us, not materially or educationally, but in their spiritual walk (Psalm 103:17,18; Isaiah 54:13; Psalm 78:1-8).[39]

৵৵৵

PRAYER

*F*ather God, thank You for giving me the desire to pray for my children and grandchildren. May I remain faithful in this discipline. I certainly can appreciate that they need to be shielded by this hedge of protection at home, school, church, friendships, and during leisure activities. Amen.

ACTION

*B*egin today to pray specifically for your children and grandchildren. Send them a note periodically letting them know you are praying for their lives.

TODAY'S WISDOM

*I*f we are willing to take hours on end to learn to play a piano, or operate a computer, or fly an airplane, it is sheer nonsense for us to imagine that we can learn the high art of getting guidance through communion with the Lord without being willing to set aside time for it. It is no accident that the Bible speaks of prayer as a form of waiting on God.

PAUL S. REES

From
Grammy's Kitchen

Rise-and-Shine Pancakes

You can make these yummy cakes in a plain round version (for practice) or in fancy star, sun, or alphabet shapes. Pour on some warm maple syrup or spread on some golden apricot jam, and you've got a perfect Saturday-morning day starter! (They're good for dinner, too.) This recipe will make pancakes for 3 or 4 people.

Ingredients

> 1 ½ cups all-purpose flour
> 1 tablespoon baking powder
> ½ teaspoon salt
> 2 tablespoons sugar
> 1 to 1 ¼ cups milk
> 1 egg
> 3 tablespoons stick butter, melted, or canola oil
> Nonstick cooking spray or oil

How to Make Them

1. Put the griddle or skillet on a stove burner and turn the heat to medium-high. Let it heat up while you mix the pancake batter.

2. Measure the flour, baking powder, salt, and sugar together in a large bowl. Use a spoon or a whisk to stir these dry ingredients together.

3. In a smaller bowl, combine the milk, egg, and

melted butter (or oil). Beat with a wire whisk until thoroughly combined.

4. With your fingers, make a little well in the flour mixture in the large bowl. Pour the milk, egg, and butter mixture into the well, then stir with the whisk until all the flour is wet.

5. Check to see if the griddle is warm enough. Sprinkle a little water on the grill, if the drops disappear within seconds, it's okay to pour batter on the grill.

6. Pour about ¼ cup of batter for each pancake. Bubbles will start to pop on the surface of the pancake. When this happens, it's time to flip over the pancake.

7. You may want to warm your plates and completed pancakes in a 200° F oven until you're ready to serve.

A Household Hint for the Kitchen

During the summer when green peppers are at good prices, buy a large supply, chopping them up and freezing in Zip-loc bags or small jars. They are ready to use for pizza, hamburgers, meatloaf, and salads.

That's My Grandma!

❧❧❧

Grandchildren are the crown of old men,
and the glory of sons is their fathers.
PROVERBS 17:6

*W*HAT A GREAT THRILL IT IS TO HEAR my children say with honor, "This is my mom." One of the Ten Commandments says that we are to honor our mothers and fathers (Exodus 20:12). We live in a time when many children and parents don't honor each other. I can't think of a more wasted life than to have children and grandchildren who don't honor their parents and grandparents. If this were true for me, I would rightly think that somewhere along the way I made some bad choices. Oh, yes, there are some children who show irreverence to parents unjustifiably, but mainly children reflect back to us how we have behaved toward them.

A good test of whether you are a grandparent who is respected is to ask yourself, "Do I want my grandson or granddaughter to grow up and be like me?"

One way we as Christians need to be a spiritual witness to the world is through the ways our families are different—that we reflect respect and honor for others.[40]

❧❧❧

PRAYER

*F*ather God, thank You for my children and grand-children. Help me make a positive impact upon their lives. May the outside world see how I respond to life in Your name. Amen.

ACTION

*B*egin investing in the lives of your grandchildren today. Determine that they will be proud to call you "Grandma."

TODAY'S WISDOM

*N*ever tell people how to do things. Tell them what to do, and they will surprise you with their ingenuity.

GENERAL GEORGE S. PATTON

SPIRIT LIFTERS

♥ Hang a basket or two—or thirty—from the ceiling beam or over a wall in the kitchen or breakfast room.

♥ Read Ecclesiastes 3—the whole chapter. List from that chapter what time in life it is for you now. What percentage of your life is available for inward pursuits?

♥ Even if you don't have children, keep a supply of cookies or Popsicles in your freezer and invite neighborhood children over regularly to talk and play. Or, when they bike by, say hello!

♥ What aspect of your home or apartment do you enjoy most—the view, the quiet, the yard? Let that be the focus of your hospitality. Share the parts of your life that bring you pleasure.

Be a Listener

❧❧❧

When there are many words, transgression is unavoidable,
but he who restrains his lips is wise.

PROVERBS 10:19

I'VE HEARD IT SAID THAT GOD GAVE US two ears and only one
mouth because He wants us to listen twice as much as we
speak. I don't know about you, but I've never had to apologize for something I haven't said. It's much easier and really
more natural for us to speak rather than to listen. Speaking
comes naturally; we have to learn to listen. It takes real discipline to keep from talking.

As a parent—and certainly as a grandparent—we need to
be known as good listeners. And while you listen, be sure to
remember there are always two sides to every story. And usually when you listen you are only hearing one version of what
happened. Postpone any judgment until you have heard *all* the
evidence—then wait some more.

Eleanor Roosevelt, in one of her many speeches stated,

> A mature person is one who does not think only in
> absolutes, who is able to be objective even when
> deeply stirred emotionally, who has learned that
> there is both good and bad in all people and in all
> things, and who walks humbly and deals charitably

with the circumstances of life. Knowing that in this world no one is all-knowing and, therefore, all of us need both love and charity.

Our Scripture verse today talks to us about being more of a listener than a talker. Too many words can lead to putting one's foot into one's mouth. The more we speak, the greater the chance of being offensive. The wise person restrains his speech. Listening seldom gets us into trouble, but our mouths certainly cause transgressions.

When listening to our grandchildren, they will tell us everything on their own. People love to talk, and when they do you sometimes hear more than you want to hear. Grandchildren love to talk to their grandparents because they feel secure and safe around you. Don't violate that trust because it is hard to regain.

PRAYER

Father God, thank You for giving me two good ears to hear. Help me be a better listener. Amen.

ACTION

Today concentrate on listening, not speaking.

TODAY'S WISDOM

You cannot receive a sincere compliment without feeling better...and just as important, you cannot give a sincere compliment without feeling better yourself!

ZIG ZIGLAR

In the Garden

❧

She turned around and saw Jesus standing there.

JOHN 20:14

*A*S A SPECIAL TREAT, I'M GOING TO let my Bob share with you today!

❧

As a boy of nine, I experienced one of my favorite bonding moments with my grandfather on my father's side. He was a robust cotton farmer with hands of steel, armor for battle, and a heart for God. Every Sunday morning while visiting our "Papa," he would take us to Anderson Chapel Methodist Church on the outskirts of Anson, Texas. One day, as we began to sing, Papa's rough voice uttered these words: "I come to the garden alone, while the dew is still on the roses, and the voice I hear falling on my ear, the Son of God discloses. And He walks with me, and He talks with me, and He tells me I am His own; and the joy we share as we tarry there, none other has ever known."

I will always remember this great scene. It made such an

impression on a young boy's heart that it has stayed with me for more than six decades.

This great gospel song, "In the Garden," was written by C. Austin Miles in 1912 after reading the Scripture where Mary Magdalene came to the garden and told the disciples that she had seen the Lord. Mr. Miles believed in meditating on Scripture. He didn't simply read a passage, but he would close his eyes and visualize the scene and even put himself in the scene. This is what he did before writing this great hymn of the church. He "saw" Mary in the garden with Jesus. This vision became words and music to what he saw.

Quite often as I work in my own garden in the cool of the morning before the noonday heat arrives, I catch myself singing the words to this beautiful hymn. The words and melody are so soothing to my spirit. I know without a doubt that God walks with me, and He talks with me, and He tells me I am His own.

I'm not even sure that Papa ever knew of the legacy he left with me. Often what we do with our grandchildren will be remembered long after we are no longer here.

PRAYER

*F*ather God, let me be sensitive regarding my lifestyle modeling around my grandchildren. My desire is to leave a positive legacy with these young ones. Amen.

ACTION

*A*sk a child what he has been doing and you may not get much of an answer. Mention a familiar TV program, and he will talk your ear off. Why not watch that program together? Then there will be plenty to talk about.

TODAY'S WISDOM

*T*he simplest toy—one which even the youngest child can operate—is called a grandparent.

They Go On
in Memory of Grandpa

*Success is to be measured not so much by
the position that one has reached in life as by the obstacles
which he has overcome while trying to succeed.*

BOOKER T. WASHINGTON

ON WHAT SHOULD HAVE BEEN one of the happiest days of his life, Chris Swan knew someone very influential was missing last Saturday during graduation ceremonies at Bellflower St. John Bosco. For Chris and his twin brother, Troy, their grandfather was the person who guided, protected, nurtured, sheltered, and willed them to succeed since they were three-year-olds.

He was in the stands in March when Chris scored 11 points and helped St. John Bosco win the Southern Section Division II-AA basketball championship. He'd watch whenever Troy ran track for the Braves.

Azzie Mitchell had little money and was in poor health because of diabetes. He and the boys lived in an apartment in South Los Angeles. They had no car, no computer, no cable television. But Azzie dedicated his life to making sure his two grandsons were focused on the future. "All these years, I've been trying to get them prepared for college."

The story of how the Swan boys had made it this far was compelling enough.

219

Chris was an honors student who completed his school reports by writing them in pen at home, then typing them on a computer in the school library. He and his brother got to school in a one-hour commute by taking the Metro Rail, then a bus. He couldn't watch college basketball games on ESPN, so he read the newspaper the next day to find out scores.

These were mere inconveniences compared to the big struggle of trying to reach college.

At age two, the boys were handed over to the Arizona social services department by their father, a man they never knew. Their mother was out of their life by age three. Both parents were involved with drugs.

Enter Azzie, who took them in, moved to Watts, and tried to teach them right from wrong.

"I had a dope dealer on one side and a gang hangout on the other side," Azzie said. "They tried to get my boys."

The boys wouldn't give in. Chris grew to 6 feet 2, became a starting guard for the Braves, scored 1,260 on the SAT, and became a school favorite because of his friendly smile and charming personality. Few knew of his plight because he refused to complain or offer excuses. Education was his ticket to a better life.

After the basketball season ended, Chris got the call he had been waiting for. The Air Force Academy wanted him. He accepted and will enroll at the Air Force prep school in July. Troy has plans to attend junior college.

From tragedy to triumph. It's been part of their lives, and it struck again last week. Just five days before high school graduation, the moment their grandfather had been waiting for, the boys received a phone call late Monday night at home from the hospital. Their grandfather had died.

"Me and my brother, we're really close," Chris said. "If there's a moment of weakness for me, he'll be strong. If he's weak, I'm there for him. Without my brother, I would have broken down." The brothers cried together on that first night. Then the St. John Bosco family of friends, teachers, and classmates intervened. They went to grad night. And they went to graduation.

With their aunt and grandmother looking on, the boys went to the podium to be recognized. Chris knew what he was going to do.

"I thought about my grandfather," he said, "but I didn't want to cry. I don't know if I've fully grasped he's not coming back, but he's not, so you have to keep going. We're stronger for what he did."

Like a guardian angel who came when needed, Azzie left before he had the chance to see his grandsons cross the finish line as high school graduates.

"That's the part that hurts the most," Chris said. "He was just a week away."

But Azzie's job was complete. He gave them hope and instilled discipline and self-confidence. The boys are on a path to college and won't forget what he did.

The twins are prepared to separate for the first time and aren't afraid of what the future has in store.

"We'll miss each other, but we know this is the best for us, to get out on our own and make men of us. Hopefully, in ten years, [me and my brother] can sit down and be satisfied with our lives," Chris said.[41]

PRAYER

*F*ather God, help me be the grandparent who will go the extra mile if called upon. I want to be dependable in the raising and influencing of my grandchildren. Give me the strength every day to meet the task before me. Amen.

ACTION

*A*sk your grandchildren (or their parents) to send you their school pictures each year. Be sure to write the date on the back of the photo and their age, city, and name of school. It's fun to see how they grow from year to year.

TODAY'S WISDOM

*T*hrow away all ambition beyond that of doing the day's work well. The travelers on the road to success live in the present, heedless of taking thought for the morrow. Live neither in the past nor in the future, but let each day's work absorb your entire energies, and satisfy your wildest ambition.

WILLIAM OSLER

A Heritage
of Gardening

*Children have never been very good at
listening to their elders, but they have
never failed to imitate them.*

JAMES BALDWIN

A GARDEN CAN HELP PEOPLE CROSS generational boundaries.
Our grandchildren love to be a part of our gardening experience. The whole process is like a living botany laboratory. And
the time we spend together working with soil and plants is a
perfect opportunity to act out one of our favorite verses of
Scripture:

> These words, which I am commanding you today,
> shall be on your heart. You shall teach them dili-
> gently to your sons and shall talk of them when
> you sit in your house and when you walk by the
> way and when you lie down and when you rise up
> (Deuteronomy 6:6-7).

We use every opportunity to teach our grandchildren about
God and creation. Their hands help till the ground, scatter the
seeds in the trenches, cover the seeds with fertile soil, and help
with the first watering. We find that children are perfect for
these chores. What child doesn't love to dig in the dirt?

Each time they visit (which is often), they can't get out of the van fast enough to see how the plants are growing. And they can hardly wait for the first harvest. Because there is always more than we need, they get to take some home for their families and also to share with neighbors.

They share the chores too—weeding, watering, picking snails. Bob often gives them one or more "I Was Caught Being Good" stickers to show his appreciation for their help. He's even been known to take them for a special treat at the local yogurt shop or hamburger stand. Our grandchildren have truly bonded with their "PaPa" by working with him in the yard and the garden.[42]

&&&

PRAYER

*F*ather God, let me be sensitive to teach my grand-children about You in every situation. All situations, good or bad, have an opportunity for learning. Let me never forget this truth. Amen.

ACTION

*I*nvolve your grandchildren in some learning experi-ences. If they live far away, give them a jingle and talk about life.

TODAY'S WISDOM

*W*e need love's tender lessons taught as only weak-nesses can; God hath his small interpreters; the child must teach the man.

JOHN GREENLEAF WHITTIER

From
Grammy's Kitchen

Good-for-You Turkey Sausage

This yummy sausage goes great with your pancakes.

Serves 4 to 6 people

Ingredients

> 1 pound ground turkey
> ½ teaspoon nutmeg
> ½ teaspoon sage
> ½ teaspoon thyme
> ⅛ teaspoon cayenne pepper (or less)
> 1 teaspoon salt

Cooking Tools

> Skillet or 9 x 13 baking pan
> Spatula
> Kitchen timer

How to Make It

1. Mix all the ingredients together—it's easier to do it with your hands. Shape the meat into 12 small patties.

2. Put the patties in an ungreased skillet and cook them over medium heat until they are brown on one side. Turn them over with the spatula to brown other side. Or put them on a baking pan and bake at 350° for 20 to 30 minutes, just until they are no

longer pink on the inside. (Cut one open with a kitchen knife to check.)

A Household Hint for the Kitchen

To quickly remove water from the lettuce greens that you have just washed, simply put into a clean pillowcase or lingerie bag and spin in your washing machine for two minutes. Remove from the bag and tear up, making a big salad. Store in a plastic bowl in the refrigerator for up to two weeks. Lettuce stays fresh and crisp.

The Freedom to Cry

༄༅

But we proved to be gentle among you,
as a nursing mother tenderly cares
for her own children.

1 THESSALONIANS 2:7

*W*HEN YOU THINK OF THE APOSTLE PAUL, you may think of the person who endured imprisonment, flogging, stoning, and shipwrecks (see 2 Corinthians 11:23-27), and that toughness was very much a part of the fiery apostle. But today's reading reveals his tender side. He describes himself as being gentle and tender. His hard-as-nails toughness didn't mean he was without his soft side.

I saw an example of a tough-but-tender man when Barbara Walters interviewed real-life hero "Stormin' Norman" Schwarzkopf, the four-star general who led the allied forces of Desert Storm to their Gulf War victory over Iraq in the 1990s. As this tough military man talked about the war, I saw tears in his eyes.

His interviewer noticed, too, and in her classic style, Barbara Walters asked, "Why, General, aren't you afraid to cry?" General Schwarzkopf replied without hesitation, "No, Barbara, I'm afraid of a man who won't cry!" This truly great man knows that being tough doesn't mean being insensitive or unfeeling or afraid to cry. No wonder soldiers gave their best when they served under his command. They knew the general cared about them; they could trust the man giving the orders. People want leaders whose hearts can be touched by our situations and who touches our hearts as well.

Perhaps you played sports when you were in high school or college. Do you remember being encouraged by your coaches? And when he or she explained the next play or the strategy for the game-winning maneuver, maybe she put her arm on your shoulder or looked you in the eye. That simple gesture said, "I believe in you. You can make it happen."

Athletics can indeed be a real source of encouragement as girls and boys travel the path to adulthood. Granted, professional sports have become larger than life with the influx of the media dollars, but athletics remain a place where we can see the tender side of a tough athlete. That's what we're looking at when we see grown folks jump into the arms of a coach or a teammate, two or more buddies high-fiving it, or a swarm of players jumping on top of the player who just made the big play. This childlike excitement is the tender side of the not-to-be-beaten athlete.

Are you able to give your grandchildren pats on the back or bear hugs? We're all on the same team—God's!—and we all need some encouragement as we head onto the field to make the big plays. We need each other if we're going to be victorious in this game called life.[43]

PRAYER

*F*ather God, I stand before You humbly, recognizing that nothing should make me arrogant or high-minded. Amen.

ACTION

*W*e can be a great inspiration to all of our grandchildren, both girls and boys. Give a pat on the back, send an e-mail, give a telephone call, or send them a note saying, "Good job." You can make a difference.

TODAY'S WISDOM

If your grandchildren are young, get on the floor and build block towers. This is the season when you are invited to read, to play, to imagine, to dream! Your lap is the "favorite place to be." Your smile is more valuable than money. Your words mean more than those on the television, in a magazine, or in a classroom. Savor the moments of this season that will never come around again.

AUTHOR UNKNOWN

Grandchildren Are
a Reward from God

✎✎✎

Children are a gift of the LORD.
PSALM 127:3

OUR GRANDCHILDREN ARE CONTINUALLY reaching out to see if
we really love them. When are we going to learn to say, "I love
you, and I am very proud of you"? They long to hear those
words, and they will continue to test us until they hear *and*
believe those words from us. What do children do?

- They yell and scream in the grocery store.
- They have temper tantrums in the restaurant.
- They wear strange clothes.
- They have funny haircuts in odd colors.
- They use vulgar language.
- They run away from home.
- They get bad grades in school.
- They run around with friends we don't approve of.

In these negative behaviors, they are indirectly asking, "Do
you approve of me?" Are they hearing your positive response?
We had a good friend whose son was not into sports and

athletics like his dad desired. The boy was into motocross racing. The parents came to our pastor, and the dad asked the pastor what he should do. The pastor, not surprisingly, said, "Take up motocrossing!" The dad predictably said, "I don't like...

- dirt
- grease
- motorcycles
- the crowd
- etc.!

The pastor replied, "How much do you love your son? Enough to get grease on your hands and clothes?" The next week the dad was off with his son to the local motocross event. Soon after they were involved with dirt, grease, and different people. Through these actions, the dad showed his son that he really loved him more than anything else, even if everything wasn't the way the dad would have liked.

We need to understand that our sons and daughters are a heritage from the Lord and that grandchildren are a reward from God. And we need to start living as though we believe it.

❧❧❧

PRAYER

*F*ather God, may You reveal to me today that my children and grandchildren are rewards from You. Sometimes I get so discouraged that I want to throw in the towel. I'm looking forward to some special encouragement from You today. Amen.

ACTION

• Write your grandchildren notes letting them know how much you love them. Give a few specific traits you like about them. (Do it even if your grandchildren are young.)

• Make a point to spend quality one-on-one time with each of your grandchildren. (Do this by phone, letter, e-mail, or video if they live away from you.)

• Place a note on your calendar next month to do it again.

TODAY'S WISDOM

*B*e the right person in the right place at the right time doing the right thing in the right way.

If I Had It All
to Do Over

੧੭੭੭

This is My body which is given for you,
do this in remembrance of Me.

LUKE 22:19

$\mathcal{E}$ACH OF US, REGARDLESS OF WHAT our ages are, look back with regret that we didn't take more time to savor and do those things that build relationships. My Bob gets melancholy when we see our old photo slides of the children when they were young. He remembers when he could have if only he would have. But we can't go back and recapture lost opportunities. We need to take advantage of each day and live it to the fullest.

When we take communion at our church, the elements are placed on a table with these words carved on the side facing the congregation: "This Do in Remembrance of Me." The Scriptures state very clearly that we are to look back to the cross and remember what Christ did for us. At the communion table we are to—

- *Break bread:* "This is My body which is given for you; do this in remembrance of Me."

- *Drink from the cup:* "This cup which is poured out for you is the new covenant in My blood."

We are to remember what Christ Jesus did for us in history. Elisabeth Elliot states, "Ultimate hatred and ultimate love met on those two crosspieces of wood. Suffering and love were brought into harmony."

As we look back over our lives, let's make sure that we have accepted Jesus as He suffered for us and our sins on the cross and paid the price of His death because of His ultimate love for us. This unselfish act was the greatest event in human history. As we look back, may we clearly remember Jesus, the bread, and the cup of wine.[44]

PRAYER

*F*ather God, help me see the important events in my life as forks in the road that made me who I am today. I want to especially thank You for reaching out to me so I could accept Jesus as my personal Messiah. In one instant I was saved in You! I have never regretted that decision. Thank You for saving my soul. Amen.

ACTION

- Write in the front of your Bible your recollection of when you became a child of God. Include date, time, place, and situation.

- If this has not happened to you, select a pastor, a friend, a neighbor, or someone who is already a child of God and ask him or her to tell you about God's salvation through Jesus.

TODAY'S WISDOM

*H*e is no fool who gives what he cannot keep to gain what he cannot lose.

JIM ELLIOT

Continue Singing
God's Song

❧❧❧

Do not grieve, for the joy of the LORD is your strength.
NEHEMIAH 8:10 NIV

THERE IS A SEASON OF LIFE THAT challenges our beliefs about the
next stage of life. The older we get, the more we wonder, *What
happens when we die?* Lee Iacocca, in his book *Straight Talk*,
has some interesting thoughts on this phase of the hereafter:

> As I get older, I think more and more about what
> comes next. I know there's got to be something
> else after this life is over, because I can't grasp the
> alternative. I can't imagine that through all eter-
> nity I'll never see anyone I love again, that my
> whole awareness will just be obliterated. I can't
> believe that we're only bodies passing through.
>
> When I muse about this, I think of all the great
> moments I had with my father. It's inconceivable
> that I had this wonderful period in life with him
> and then suddenly the curtain dropped. Instead, I
> want to believe I'm going to meet up with him
> again. I also want to have the opportunity to catch
> up with Mary, if only to tell her what I forgot to

tell her, and to meet all my lifelong friends who have died. I do think they're out there someplace.

I haven't yet formed a clear idea about what the hereafter might be like. I don't know if everyone's an angel. Or an apparition. Or it's just all beyond comprehension. But I do hope that it's going to be better than here, because life on this planet is not exactly peaches and cream. I mean, this life is tough. I suppose that's the promise religion holds out. If you can take this life as it comes and give it your best, there will be something better afterwards.

I've always marveled at how belief in the hereafter gets accentuated as people grow older. Until their deathbeds, many of the great minds in science thought that because their soul and being were wrapped up in their body—the old ninety-eight cents worth of chemicals—and that because after death these would no longer be a body, that was it. But now when they have to go, suddenly they want to believe in somebody up there because they don't know where they're going and they are scared.[45]

If you haven't prepared for what happens next, you might want to read the following Scriptures to help you arrive at a point of belief.

- Romans 3:23
- Romans 6:23
- Acts 16:30-31
- Ephesians 2:8-9
- Romans 10:9-10

- Luke 18:13
- Luke 23:43
- John 10:28
- John 14:2-3
- John 3:16

You can receive Jesus right now by faith through prayer!

Lord Jesus,

I need You. Thank You for dying on the cross for my sins. I open the door of my life and receive You as my Savior and Lord. Thank You for forgiving my sins and giving me eternal life. Take control of the throne of my life. Make me the kind of person You want me to be.[46]

If you prayed this prayer, read the following Scriptures for further assurance.

- Revelation 3:20
- 1 John 1:9
- 1 John 5:11-13
- Hebrews 13:5
- John 14:21

PRAYER

*F*ather God, thank You for letting me be Your child now and forever. Amen.

ACTION

*I*f you have never prayed a prayer of salvation before and you want to now, kneel before God and repeat the simple prayer shared in this devotion.

TODAY'S WISDOM

*T*herefore, I tell you, whatever you ask for in prayer, believe that you have received it, and it will be yours.

MARK 11:24 NIV

SPIRIT LIFTERS

♥ Celebrate your memories. Choose one day a year to gather and look through photo albums, show slides, and watch home videos.

♥ Let down your hair and play games like tag and hide-and-seek as a family. Modify the rules, if you have to, so that all ages can join in—and remember to have fun!

♥ Light a candle by the kitchen sink. The soft light can add a spirit of loveliness even to a messy countertop.

♥ Parsley in a jar of water in the refrigerator looks inviting to those who open it. I also enjoy keeping a "bouquet" of parsley on the windowsill by the sink.

Being a Feminine Grandmother

❧❧❧

All beautiful you are, my darling; there is no flaw in you.
SONG OF SONGS 4:7 NIV

ONE OF THE MOST BEAUTIFUL TIMES of a woman's life is when she becomes a grandmother. Often we don't think so because we get discouraged by the media's ideal of a woman, but as we mature, God's idea of being a feminine woman blossoms.

When I was a little girl, I used to dream of being a "lady." The world of *Little Women,* with its gracious manners and old-fashioned, flowing dresses, fascinated me. Softness and lace, tantalizing fragrance and exquisite texture, a nurturing spirit and a love of beauty—these images of femininity shaped my earliest ideas of loveliness.

Is that kind of femininity a lost value today? I don't believe so. The world has changed, and most of us live in simple skirts or business suits or jeans instead of flowing gowns. But I still believe that somewhere in the heart of most of us is a little girl who longs to be a lady.

I also believe that today's world is hungering to be transformed by femininity. What better antidote for an impersonal and violent society than warm, gentle, feminine strength?

What better cure for urban sprawl and trashed-out countrysides than a love of beauty and a confidence in one's ability to make things lovely? What better hope for the future than a nurturing mother's heart that is more concerned for the next generation than for its own selfish desires? All these qualities—gentle strength, love of beauty, care and nurturing—are part of femininity.

Being a woman created by God is such a privilege—and the gift of our femininity is something we can give both to ourselves and to the people around us. Just one flower can warm up a cold, no-nonsense atmosphere with an aura of "I care." Women have always had the ability to transform an environment, to make it comfortable and inviting. I believe we should rejoice in that ability and make the most of it.

This doesn't mean we have to follow a set pattern or adopt a cookie-cutter style. The specific expressions of femininity vary greatly. When I think "feminine," I usually think of soft colors, lace, and flowers. I love ruffled curtains and flower-sprigged wallpaper, delicate bone china, and old-fashioned garden prints. And I feel especially beautiful when I'm dressed up in soft and colorful fabrics.

But I know women with vastly different styles who still exude that special quality I call femininity—women who wear their tailored tweeds or their casual cottons (or their gardening "grubbies") with an air of gentleness and sensitivity. Women who fill their sleek modern kitchens or their utilitarian office cubicles with that unmistakable sense of warmth, caring, and responsiveness. Women who combine self-confidence and an indomitable spirit with a gracious humility and a tender teachability. Women who wear femininity with the grace and confidence with which they wear their favorite elegant scent.

Femininity is so many things. To me, it is objects chosen for their beauty as well as their usefulness...and lovingly cared for. It is people accepted and nurtured, loveliness embraced and shared. More important, femininity is the spirit of care and compassion. In my mind, the most feminine woman is one with an eye and ear for others and a heart for God.

At its best, our femininity arises naturally out of who we are and finds its natural expression in the way we live our lives and make our homes. But in our hectic, hard-driving society, it's easy to lose track of our gentle, feminine side. Femininity is something we must nurture in ourselves and in our homes and celebrate as God's gift to us.

Femininity can be cultivated in many ways. A fragrant oil or a few drops of perfume in bathwater. A daisy on your desk. A lace scarf or an embroidered hanky in your pocket. A crocheted shawl around your shoulders. Whatever awakens the calm and gentle spirit within you will nurture the spirit of loveliness in your life.

The expression of femininity is very personal. It's an expression of a woman's unique self. It is closely tied with identity and with style. Many of the most feminine women I know develop a signature or trademark that marks their distinctiveness. One woman always wears hats. Another enhances her distinctive presence with a favorite fragrance. Still another adopts a theme or motif that becomes part of her identity.

Femininity includes a wholesome sensuality—a rejoicing in the fragrances and textures and sounds of God's world. We honor God and express the spirit of femininity when we get excited.

I make the effort to surround myself with beauty. When I do, I feel more beautiful. I experience the joy of sharing beauty with those closest to me. And I am motivated to reach out to others with gentleness and care.

The true spirit of femininity comes from the *heart,* and I

nurture it when I pay attention to what is truly important in life. That's why I need the message of 1 Peter 3:3-5 NIV:

> Your beauty should not come from outward adornment, such as braided hair and the wearing of gold jewelry and fine clothes. Instead, it should be that of your inner self, the unfading beauty of a gentle and quiet spirit, which is of great worth in God's sight. For this is the way the holy women of the past who put their hope in God used to make themselves beautiful.

As women of God, we are the pacesetters for femininity. Read the book of Solomon (sometimes called the Song of Songs), and you will be amazed at how we can live with what God has given us as women. Don't sell yourself short. Reflect in your presence what God intended you to be.

PRAYER

*F*ather God, You know that my heart's desire is to be a godly woman, someone other women see as a reflection of what You describe in Scripture as a beautiful woman. Show me Your ways today. Let me be that beautiful fragrance that others want to sense. Amen.

ACTION

*W*rite in your journal what makes you feel feminine.

TODAY'S WISDOM

*B*eauty is the only thing that time cannot harm. Philosophies fall away like sand, and creeds follow one another like the withered leaves of Autumn; but what is beautiful is a joy for all seasons and a possession for all eternity.

OSCAR WILDE

□　□　□

Living a Life
of Successes

୨୧୨୧

The pride of your heart has deceived you, you who live in the
clefts of the rocks and make your home on the heights, you who
say to yourself, "Who can bring me down to the ground?"

OBADIAH 1:3 NIV

*O*NE OF THE ADVANTAGES OF BEING more mature in age is that
we can look back at the choices we made along the way—
some failures but mostly successful. We begin to form an
idea in our mind about this important question, What is
success?

A few summers ago our family rented a modest cabin at
Lake Arrowhead in the San Bernardino mountains, about one
hour from our home. It was going to be a quiet getaway to
read, rest, and relax. We don't get to do these three R's enough.

During the course of the three days up there, my attention
was drawn to a dusty old framed verse that skipped my attention until day two. It hung in one of the bathrooms, and as I
took time to read it, my eyes came across this collection of
thoughts on success:

> Great people are just ordinary people with an extra-
> ordinary amount of determination....There is no
> gain without pain. When you fail to plan, you plan

to fail....Change your thoughts and you can change your world. There are infinite possibilities in little beginnings if God is in them. Build a dream and the dream will build you. Inch by inch, anything is a cinch. I am God's project, and God never fails. Don't let impossibilities intimidate you, do let possibilities motivate you. Make your decisions on "God's ability," not your ability. What you are is God's gift to you; what you make of yourself is your gift to God. It's possible to face the music with God's song in your heart. God's delays are not God's denials. I'd rather attempt to do something great and fail than attempt to do nothing and succeed....Look at what you have left, not at what you have lost. Find a hurt and heal it. You are God's project and God never fails.[47]

As I finished reading these collections of clever thoughts, I began to think upon this concept of success. Today our media tries to bombard us with all the materialism of the universe to make us compare our adventure with all the world has to offer. My first thoughts were that if material success brought happiness then all the wealthy people of the world would be very happy and all the poor people would be very sad, but that's really the opposite of what I've observed in life.

I asked myself, "Then what is success?" A quote from the past flashed through my brain: "Success is progressive realization of worthwhile goals!" Yes, that's the whole idea of success. That must mean we have to sit down and think through some worthwhile goals, and we must attain them over a period of time. They aren't instantly attainable; they are progressively realized—postponed gratifications, if you will.

Two common barriers that prevent most people from reaching their goals are: 1) We have made a habit of past failures and mistakes, and 2) We fear failure. Because of these two negatives, many of us never reach our potential.

As you think through today's thoughts, you may want to do some homework on your definition of success. And even though we are grandparents, there is a lot of living to be experienced. Don't become a couch potato. Write down what you want to accomplish in the next five years, and get started!

❧❧

PRAYER

*F*ather God, I am thankful that I know and put my trust in You. You are awesome and almighty. I look to You for guidance in my life. May my later years be purpose driven. Amen.

ACTION

*S*it down and write out two goals for each of the following areas of your life:

- spiritual
- professional
- financial
- family

- home
- leisure
- health

TODAY'S WISDOM

*S*uccess is neither fame, wealth, nor power; rather it is seeking, knowing, loving, and obeying God. If you seek, you will know; if you know, you will love; if you love, you will obey.

CHARLES MALIR

Do You Care?

❧❧❧

But prove yourselves doers of the word,
and not merely hearers who delude themselves.
JAMES 1:22

As GRANDPARENTS, WE HAVE a wonderful opportunity to "walk our talk." These precious youngsters watch every step we take and every word we utter. They are looking to see if Grandma and Grandpa are real. Can we be trusted. If so, they will respond in a very favorable way; if not, they will be guarded and standoffish. Young children have a great discernment with first impressions. When our daughter, Jenny, was very young, she had great discernment when she first met someone. We were astonished at how accurate her observations were.

Grandchildren cry out, "Do you care?" If we care, they can be inspired and brought to a higher level when they are around us. We are called to step out from the ordinary path of life to impact these grandchildren God has brought into our presence.

When we review history, we are brought face-to-face with great men and women who accomplished significant things. What did they possess? They each had a vision, and once challenged, they followed through on their calling. They didn't just say "I love you; I care for you," and then fall away from that passion. They went the extra mile to really care. That's the challenge we face as grandparents. Do we care enough to make a difference? None of us realizes the plan God has for the youngsters in our care. We might be encouraging a future president, a future business leader, a future teacher, a future attorney, a future husband, a future wife. Whatever their calling, we, as grandparents, have a great influence on how they will approach that vocation.

Sometimes in each of our lives we have been challenged to do something great—maybe at a retreat, by a powerful sermon, by a pastor, by a television program, by a Sunday school teacher, by a teacher in school, or by an inspirational coach. Maybe this impact has made a real difference in your life, but then maybe you've never gone beyond the commitment or thought stage. Now is the time to act.

In today's passage, James tells us not to merely listen to the Word but to do what it says. Be challenged today to work out your love by caring for those around you. Don't be known as just a hearer of the Word, but be a doer. It takes a lot of effort and sacrifice, and not always doing what you want to do. It costs time and money, and often being disappointed by expecting too much. One of the Barnes' mottoes is: "The greater the expectations, the greater disappointments when they aren't met."

PRAYER

*F*ather God, let my life show to my grandchildren that I really care. Let them know that I truly love them. May my life reflect the teaching of Your Word. May I truly be a doer of Your commands and principles. Amen.

ACTION

*W*rite in your journal three desires you have to serve each of your grandchildren.

TODAY'S WISDOM

*S*aying "Yes!" to God is not a simple matter because making our lives into lives of love is not a simple or easy thing. To choose love as a life principle means that my basic mind-set or question must be: What is the loving thing to be, to do, to say? My consistent response to each of life's events, to each person who enters and touches my life, to each demand on my time and nerves and heart, must somehow be transformed into an act of love. However, in the last analysis, it is this "Yes!" that opens me to God. Choosing love as a life principle widens the chalice of my soul, so that God can pour into me His gifts and graces and powers.

JOHN POWELL

Be a Healer
of Divisions

If a house is divided against itself,
that house will not be able to stand.
MARK 3:25

*I*N AN IDEAL WORLD, WE WOULD HAVE no division in our homes
and families. But since we don't live in a perfect world, there
are divisions. The number one divider is divorce. In the
United States, half the families are under the dark cloud of
divorce. In my own family, my son and daughter have experienced that division. As grandparents, our hearts ache for
both families. We have a special sensitivity for our five grandchildren. When divorce occurs, it changes the whole dynamics
of the family structure.

Today the family unit is under great stress, and many families are falling victim to separation. Because of this we find
many victims lying by the wayside due to the powerful forces
of Satan.

Abraham Lincoln said when he accepted the nomination
for a United States Senate seat, "Either the opponents of
slavery will arrest the further spread of it and place it where
the public mind shall rest in the belief that it is in the course
of ultimate extinction, or its advocates will push it forward till

it shall become alike lawful in all the states, old as well as new—north as well as south." Lincoln's stand against slavery and for the equality of all people resulted in his defeat in the election, but Lincoln responded philosophically: "Though I now sink out of view and shall be forgotten, I believe I have made some marks which will tell for the cause of civil liberty long after I am gone." Well, Lincoln certainly didn't "sink out of view"! After being elected president later, he worked to bring together those who had been at war and to heal the hurts that had divided the nation. Lincoln knew that a house divided could not stand.

Many families today are divided and need to be brought back together; many hurts in those families need to be healed. With my own children we witnessed separation, but it also occurred in my extended family. Two of my aunts, who were sisters, didn't speak to each other for ten years. The initial disagreement, as slight as it may have been, became unbridgeable. But separation or brokenness doesn't have to be permanent. Neither of my aunts would apologize or admit to being wrong. Having watched this go on for a long time, I finally decided to be the peacemaker. I arranged a family gathering and invited both aunts together. After just a short time, the two began to open up and talk to each other. By the end of the evening, they had made amends, and they were able to enjoy the last 15 years of their lives together. Although reconciliation may not always be possible, healing from the wounds is available through Christ.

Maybe divisions exist in your family. If so, know that the warning in today's Scripture is for you: "If a house is divided against itself, that house will not be able to stand." What can you do to help bring unity to your family? Whatever steps you decide to take, know that you'll need much patience and many prayers. As you seek God's blessing on your endeavors to encourage the ones you love, ask God to give you wisdom, patience, and understanding. Know, too, that it will take time to rebuild what has been destroyed by division. Don't feel that the situation must be resolved quickly. Be willing to walk by faith, not by sight, and pray earnestly for healing each step of the way.

As someone who has experienced the ups and downs of life, you can be a real balm of healing. Open your arms with love and welcome all into your comfort. How you treat and relate to this division and the people involved will determine how effective you can be in the healing process. Remember that every difference has two sides. Be willing to know both.

PRAYER

Father God, use me as a healer in my family. Use me to help bring unity where there is now division. Show me the steps to take. I thank You that You will be with me and my family members as we build bridges and learn to forgive one another. Amen.

ACTION

Ask your spouse to join you in praying about this situation and the goal of unity within the family.

TODAY'S WISDOM

The first thing I do, after having asked in a few words the Lord's blessing upon his precious Word, is to begin to meditate on the Word of God, searching as it were into every verse to get blessing out of it...for the sake of obtaining food for my soul. The result I have found to be almost invariably this, that after a very few minutes my soul has been led to confession, or to thanksgiving, or to intercession, or to supplication, so that, though I did not, as it were, give myself to prayer but to meditation, it had turned almost immediately more or less into prayer.

GEORGE MUELLER

Notes

1. Lee Iacocca, *Talking Straight* (New York: Bantam, 1988), p. 17.

2. Emilie Barnes, *Minute Meditations for Healing and Hope* (Eugene, OR: Harvest House Publishers, 2003), pp. 95-96.

3. Bob and Emilie Barnes, *Minute Meditations on Prayer* (Eugene, OR: Harvest House Publishers, 2003), pp. 129-30, adapted.

4. Bob Barnes, *Minute Meditations for Men* (Eugene, OR: Harvest House Publishers, 1998), pp. 249-50, adapted.

5. Bill Bright, "Four Spiritual Laws" (Arrowhead Springs, CA: Campus Crusade for Christ International, 1965).

6. Author unknown.

7. Cookie Strickland, "A Special Tribute" *Keeping Hearts and Home* magazine, vol. 2, no. 3, Summer 2004, p. 36. Used by permission.

8. Bob and Emilie Barnes, *15-Minute Devotions for Couples* (Eugene, OR: Harvest House Publishers, 1995), pp. 95-96, adapted.

9. Alan Toy McGinnis, *The Friendship Factor* (Minneapolis: Augsburg, 1979), p. 23.

10. Author unknown.

11. Elon Foster, ed., *Six Thousand Sermon Illustrations* (Grand Rapids, MI: Baker Book House, 1992), p. 353.

12. Bob and Emilie Barnes, *Minute Meditations on Prayer,* pp. 121-22, adapted.

13. Received via e-mail. Author unknown.

14. Bob and Emilie Barnes, *15-Minute Devotions for Couples,* pp. 139-41, adapted.

15. Emilie Barnes, *Minute Meditations for Healing & Hope,* pp. 15-16, adapted.

16. Gary J. Oliver, "Black-and-White Living in a Gray World," in *Seven Promises of a Promise Keeper,* edited and published by Focus on the Family. Copyright © 1994, Promise Keepers. All rights reserved. International copyright secured. Used by permission.

17. Bob Barnes, *15 Minutes Alone with God for Men* (Eugene, OR: Harvest House Publishers, 1995), pp. 263-65, adapted.

18. From a Kay Arthur newsletter, reprinted in Emilie Barnes, *Minute Meditations for Healing & Hope,* pp. 99-100. Used by permission.

19. Received via e-mail. Author unknown.

20. Emilie Barnes, *15 Minutes Alone with God,* pp. 18-19, adapted.

21. Bob and Emilie Barnes, *Minute Meditations on Prayer,* pp. 103-04, adapted.

22. Emilie Barnes, *Minute Meditations for Busy Moms,* p. 43, adapted.

23. Bob Barnes, *Minute Meditations for Men,* p. 236, adapted.

24. Bob Barnes, *Minute Meditations for Men,* pp. 108-09, adapted.

25. Bob and Emilie Barnes, *15-Minute Devotions for Couples,* pp. 77-80, adapted.

26. Bob Barnes, *Minute Meditations for Men,* p. 221, adapted.

27. Author unknown.

28. Received via e-mail. Author unknown.

29. Received via e-mail. Author unknown.

30. Emilie Barnes, *15 Minutes Alone with God,* Special Olympics, 1976, Spokane, WA, pp. 73-75, adapted.

31. Taken from a tract printed and distributed by the American Tract Society, Garland, Texas.

32. Bob Barnes, *Minute Meditations for Men,* pp. 276-77, adapted.

33. Bob Barnes, *Minute Meditations for Men,* p. 178, adapted.

34. Bob Barnes, *Minute Meditations for Men,* pp. 181-82, adapted.

35. Bob Barnes, *Minute Meditations for Men,* pp. 156-57, adapted.

36. Emilie Barnes, *15 Minutes Alone with God,* pp. 100-01.

37. Bob and Emilie Barnes, *Minute Meditations on Prayer,* pp. 196-97, adapted.

38. Emilie Barnes, *Minute Meditations for Healing and Hope,* p. 75, adapted.

39. Resource material from Campus Crusade for Christ International (adapted).

40. Bob Barnes, *Minute Meditations for Men,* p. 53, adapted.

41. Eric Sondheimer, *L.A. Times,* Tuesday, June 3, 2003, Section D12, adapted.

42. Emilie Barnes, *The Spirit of Loveliness* (Eugene, OR: Harvest House Publishers, 1992), pp. 62-63, adapted.

43. Bob Barnes, *Minute Meditations for Men,* pp. 200-01, adapted.

44. Emilie Barnes, *15 Minutes of Peace with God* (Eugene, OR: Harvest House Publishers, 1997), pp. 47-48, adapted.

45. Lee Iacocca, *Straight Talk* (New York: Bantam, 1988), p. 27.

46. Bill Bright, *Four Spiritual Laws* (San Bernardino, CA: Campus Crusade for Christ, Inc., 1965), p. 10.

47. Author unknown, reprinted in Bob and Emilie Barnes, *15-Minute Devotions for Couples,* pp. 11-14.